DARK PSYCHOLOGY & MANIPULATION

The secret guide to learning the art of persuasion, how to influence people, mind control, body language, NLP secrets and hypnosis techniques

By

Fred Hansen

utilization or maltreatment of any approaches, procedures, or bearings contained inside is the singular and articulate duty of the Beneficiary peruser. By no means will any legitimate obligation or fault be held against the distributor for any reparation harms, or fiscal misfortune because of the data in this, either straightforwardly or in a roundabout way. Individual creators possess all copyrights not held by the distributor.

The data thus is offered for instructive Purposes exclusively and is all-inclusive as so. The introduction of the information is without an agreement or on the other hand, any assurance affirmation.

The trademarks that are utilized are with no consent, and the production of the trademark is without authorization or support by the trademark proprietor. All trademarks and brands inside this book are for explaining purposes and are claimed by the proprietors themselves, not subsidiary with this report

DISCLAIMER

All intellect contained in this Book is given for Enlightening and informative purposes as it were. The creator isn't in any capacity responsible for any outcomes or on the other hand, results that exude from utilizing this material.

Important endeavors have been made to give data that is both precise and successful, yet the creator isn't destined for the precision or use/abuse of this data.

FOREWARD

To start with, I will jump at the chance to thank you for venturing out of confiding in me and choosing to buy/read this Life-changing eBook. Thanks for spending your time and resources on this material. I can assure you of exact results if you will diligently follow the precise blueprint, I lay bare in the information manual you are currently reading. It has transformed lives, and I firmly believe it will equally change your own life too. All the information I presented in this Do It yourself the piece is easy to digest and practice.

TABLE OF CONTENTS

INTRODUCTION

We should start by seeing how to perceive the "dark side" of psychological thinking and behavior. We need a measure to perceive what is standard and what is considered peculiar behavior. Our first measure is the social standard. In every society, this suggests normal behavior that is considered regular, in different conditions that nullify our wisdom. For example, in Western culture, fiercely striking another person is considered a crime and an upsetting speak to a quiet society. Regardless, we suffer violence when an individual is embraced by the system, for example, a warrior caught in a war, a cop endeavoring to catch an unsafe hoodlum, a resident shielding his family from a risk. Really Another individual may misconstrue these twofold benchmarks. A warrior who does monstrosities, for instance, butcher, is a cop who uses fierceness to undermine an eyewitness by tending to or examining a resident who ignores another person's benefits in order to strengthen their position, one way or the other.

The ensuing measure is acceptable? How might we as a society pick what is right or wrong, who can pick these rights if the laws follow a moral conviction or become the security of the weak against the strong or the rich against the poor? By far most in society agree that butchering another person is against the moral law. It is simply misguided to kill him, and he ought to be repelled by the exhibition of a comparable gravity of a territory of society credited to the great legal position constrained on the dominant part by authorities. For most social requests, it was a code of exacting direct, for instance, the 10 Commandments of the Christian certainty and other Buddhist codes in the Muslim Quran. Trust in divine prize and control is reflected in the real language and laws as the reason of each edified nation. In the wake of enduring these principles, for what reason do people unshakably go off to some faraway place from this moral code, laws, and severe guidelines that license us to live in a peaceful society spoke to by agreed benchmarks of behavior that safe people?against hazard, injury, and misuse?

The third area of behavior is one not communicated in the law or in severe thoughts,

2

yet in customary behavior packs that the English would call "customs" or "mindfulness." Conduct or lead unsurprising with behavior recognized as a superior individual from a society known than act in the association of others, as demonstrated by a ton of concludes that are considered a sign of bleeding edge human progression. This is to a great extent saw on the characteristic of good behavior or when a man clears the path for a woman and permits her to start, seeing the male commitment to make sure about and shield women. Today, in specific social orders, women's benefits are tried by the customs of a sexist woman and right now of her self-sufficiency. Nevertheless, moral quality is moreover considered a sign of thriving at the most raised degrees of society, be it the English show or the Japanese lunch service.

By describing social requests in different strategies for assessing behavior through commendable laws, moral laws, or social guidelines, people regardless of everything face a wide extent of non-reasonable behaviors that consistently impact and effect others. Show where the makers of these behaviors consider themselves to be outlaws, moral codes, and the quality of the rest of society. To a great extent thusly, we all in all see that we have upset these standards, which are basic to a productive advancement. In any case, others don't consider how to treat the severity, devastation, and downfall of others as simply the choice to live without these benchmarks and the chance to continue with a questionable life. just for what they have to guarantee, have or pound.

POSITIVE PSYCHOLOGY

This examination study identifies the standards, history and hypotheses of positive psychology. It additionally breaks down ebb and flow look into on positive psychology. At last, it shows how these ideas can be used by and by, even in associations.

Exploring the historical backdrop of positive psychology, Dr Martin Seligman is the satisfaction educator and the informal dad of positive psychology, the disputable investigation of human bliss. Humanistic Abraham Maslow, in his 1954 book about inspiration and character originally used the term positive psychology. Martin Seligman made it the subject of his presidency of the American Psychological Association in 1998. He guaranteed psychology up to then was noting no and I, rather than yes and we. Persuading individuals to be useful is a superior indicator of expanded duty and love than showing individuals how to battle. William James contended that so as to contemplate ideal human working completely, one needs to consider the abstract understanding of a person.

For that conviction, in 1906, James is considered, by certain analysts, to be America's first positive therapist. Prior impacts on positive psychology originated from philosophical and strict sources. The old Greeks had numerous ways of thinking. During the Renaissance, independence began to be esteemed. Utilitarian scholars, for example, John Stuart Mill, accepted that ethical activities are those activities that boost joy for the most number of individuals, and that an exact study of satisfaction figure out which activities are good. Thomas Jefferson and different democrats accepted that Life, freedom and the quest for joy are basic rights, and that it justifies the oust of the administration. The Romantics esteemed individual enthusiastic articulation and looked for their passionate genuine selves.

As indicated by Dr. Seligman, during difficult occasions, qualities and positive feelings assist individuals with traversing. Seligman characterizes a "decent life" by using own qualities reliably. Work, administration, foundations and culture are interrelated and fundamental to positive psychology. Regardless of whether individuals were monetarily free, individuals would in any case accomplish something with their time, in the wake of getting all the enjoyment and travel out of their framework. In this manner, joy at work moves and adds to individuals' life satisfaction. Work normally shapes individuals' system or hover of impact, as people like to gather up with individuals who share shared traits with their work, industry, and expert encounters.

People can likewise consider times when they were not animated busy working; their work was monotonous and futile. Studies have indicated that the laborers, who flourish, are the ones who are consistently tested in important manners, so work can get fun and play. Besides, an ever increasing number of academic articles pressure the significance of bliss grinding away and gradually more associations are acknowledging it and make it their objective and crucial representatives. To make positive establishments, it is significant not to keep insider facts, following a crucial have viable peaceful settlements aptitudes. As indicated by Seligman, there are five qualities to positive establishments: keep developing, CEO demonstrated, being greater than its wholes of the parts, enabling to decide, and being clear with the crucial reason. Positive pioneers make positive organizations and foundations. Once more, positively and positive vitality is infectious, because, from a quantum material science viewpoint, everything is vitality.

Accordingly, individuals will in general float towards other positive individuals, positive pioneers, positive groups, foundations and positive societies. The proposed model to connect positive psychology and business, to make organizations fruitful and manageable, is to base them on the VIA Human Strengths. Foundations or associations are viewed as miniaturized scale society and small scale networks that grow outward. Originating from quality or love, versus need or dread, consistently delivers much better outcomes and results. Change is about quality. These standards could be abridged by saying that it is ideal to see, center around and draw out the best in individuals. These standards are valid across different societies around the world. Good faith for the future diminishes anxiety. Trust in life after death helps adapting to death; however refusal of life after death helps celebrating and acknowledging life more. The pith of joy is enjoying the present. The idea of time everlasting or eternality helps esteeming life, as there would be no motivation to keep something of no worth.

Positive psychology examines satisfaction and how that identifies with affection and appreciation. What confidence offers, for example, network, appreciation, absolution, reason, acknowledgment, philanthropy, and time everlasting, expands prosperity. Marriage is the expectation for joy. We pick a vocation, or fly thinking, trusting, or having confidence. The possibility for blunder in confidence makes people unassuming and open to trust that feeds love and joy.

Positive psychology additionally examines importance and inspiration and how these identify with joy. Life intention is the importance and bearing of one's world or experience and objective creation and interest. Quality relations and quality life are accomplished through arrangement of misfortunes. To comprehend whether a political activity is fortunate or unfortunate, it is conceivable to take a gander at inspiration or the thought process, for example, the general gathering/open great purposive and submitted guideline, versus an individual self-need.

Perusing articles on positive psychology, proof shows confident people lead more beneficial, not so much distressing, but rather more effective lives than cynics (Weisberg, 2010). Positive psychology contemplates the intensity of idealism and its relationship to more versatility and wellbeing. Flexibility is exemplified in the book of Viktor Frankl about a man in scan for significance. Frankl contemplated why a portion of his kindred death camp mates made it like him and other didn't, given a similar steady conditions. Frankl would have liked to see his wife once more. Specialist J. Nardini, another camp survivor guaranteed: "It was critical to think about one's self as better than what the earth inferred." According to Martin Seligman, good faith permits to conquer difficulties. Seligman depicts cynicism or surrendering as educated powerlessness. Administrators with a positive mentality settled on preferable choices over different associates. Mediators with positive outward appearances were bound to pick up concessions than the individuals who with a poker face. "Inspiration" creates less pressure related hormones, and lessens provocative responses to push.

Here is a brilliant utilization of positive psychology. IntenSati is a high-vitality cardio exercise that consolidates positive psychology. Positive certifications, balance work and feel-great talk, go with the activities with topics for care, positive psychology and the law of fascination. Moreno made this brain/body wellness routine subsequent to battling with her weight. Members consume around 800 calories for each class. The class begins with warm up reciting, "This week, who are you turning out to be? I assume liability for my contemplations and activities, consistently, in a genuine way; I co-make my world ". Each posture has a revelation. The mood of the words makes a succession of developments. Members of any age love it. Music is out of sight. "I am turning into all I need to be! I feel my joy and force. It feels so great. I am ablaze!" Some instances of development names are: significance, valiant and effortlessness.

Positive psychology shows how satisfaction or hopefulness, positive feelings and influence are useful, prompting better wellbeing and more noteworthy achievement. Glad, or positive, individuals are progressively fruitful busy working. Positive psychology proposes mind over issue. Alumni of University of Pennsylvania in positive psychology coauthored a well known business self improvement guide, established a counseling gathering to carry positive psychology into the state funded schools, through workshops on such points as estimating and supporting character qualities and temperances and learning apparatuses for building good faith and versatility. Most chances of applied positive psychology are in hierarchical counseling and business training.

Another use of positive psychology is found in wellbeing instructing. Wellbeing mentors use understanding actuation, persuasive talking and positive psychology to evoke behavior change, guarantee customers oversee themselves and positively sway wellbeing. The Patient Activation Measure (PAM) is a scale that gets some information about their convictions, information and certainty of wellbeing behaviors. Inspirational meeting aptitudes can give a central structure to wellbeing training communication. Positive psychology joins positive feelings and prosperity with both wellbeing and life span. Training psychology investigates the customer's psychological state and state of being. Positive psychology is used in instructing customers to identify life gives that are shielding them from being their best self in overseeing organ and weight issues. Wellbeing and joy are related. Instructing is scholarly exercise. Not practicing can prompt melancholy. PAM is used in walking and phone training programs. Drawn in customers are propelled. Clinical and business fields acknowledge wellbeing instructing. It is gainful to have essential consideration suppliers who can mentor.

Positive psychology additionally focuses on making versatility and positive mentalities as opposed to restoring passionate issues. Numerous individuals are discontent with their employments, and they additionally fear losing them, because of an absence of certainty. To assemble self-assurance, it is critical to be a hopeful person, to get through feelings of trepidation and make a move, be encompassed with positive individuals and to be guided. At long last, it is urgent to turn into a guide to help other people. Everybody has realized what that can exceptionally profit others. Marshall Goldsmith, well known official mentor encourages to locate a positive soul toward what the individual is doing now, that begins from inside. It is conceivable to make a positive soul by turning out to be progressively self-assured. Fruitful individuals are self-assured and confident people. They face their feelings of trepidation and act, encircle themselves with positive individuals, discover tutors and become coaches.

Positive clinicians apply best in class psychological research to individuals' lives. Positive Psychology goes past beating the despondency of past issues. Positive analysts center around where individuals need to go in their lives so they can enable them to arrive. An early piece of the change procedure is instruction. Finding out about progress and individual satisfaction is the beginning stage because it shifts the customer's outlook. As Einstein stated, individuals can't take care of issues with a similar brain that made them. Positive clinicians connect with customers to move them from enduring to flourishing, with new encounters. Something else, the individual stays stuck on old projects and biased examples of working. This action creates a positive initial step.

Positive clinicians' direction to live as per the rules that examination shows fruitful. A portion of these standards include enthusiasm for accomplishing positive results, carrying a wealth of positive vitality to connections, confronting difficulties with good faith, using qualities to accomplish objectives, renewing vitality to meet objectives, and having any kind of effect on the planet. If positive therapists have encountered and taken in these standards, it is simpler for them to guide others to do likewise and be the change they need to find on the planet, similar to Gandhi educated us. Positive therapists ask: What is the fantasy? Who may have the option to help arrive? What difficulties will there be? What qualities will defeat those difficulties? By what means will the positive vitality be kept to arrive at objectives?

What will the accomplishment of the fantasy cause on the planet? Change begins by edifying individuals. After the principal positive psychology meeting or meeting, customers comprehend that it is conceivable to acquire a positive result because their experience was outside of their standard. Customers are urged to encounter something new to end their battles. The therapist offers demonstrated methodologies to assist customers with understanding their objectives. Every meeting estimates progress. Positive therapists are guides. To accomplish bona fide satisfaction, individuals must put a similar degree of time and vitality into progressing in the direction of ideal working. To improve their lives, individuals must learn specific positive ways and recommendations of reacting to their interests, questions, tensions and reactions. They need ceaseless consolation to use their qualities, think hopefully around difficulties, and remain positive in their connections.

Some different utilizations of positive psychology comprise of focusing on a couple of things that worked out positively during the, prior day rest, builds prosperity. Asking what functions admirably and for what good reason brings out amazing arrangements. Positive psychology depends on genuine scientific research.

A focal subject of study in positive psychology, as referenced previously, is appreciation. Appreciation can amplify bliss and the great. Positive psychology can prompt a solid and upbeat harmony among work and life. The requests of shuffling work and home lead numerous ladies to attempt to do everything. In the push to be superwomen, numerous ladies dismiss what makes them glad and they neglect to acknowledge how significant their satisfaction is to being a decent specialist and a decent mother. The way to being the best at all that one does is to deal with satisfaction the manner in which wellbeing is dealt with, through cognizant decisions consistently. Individuals can use positive psychology to shift from a shortage attitude to a wealth mindset for working environment achievement. This helps taking advantage of the feeling of joy each day for possess joy and the satisfaction of those around.

It is essential to have all the things that truly matter. Cathy L. Greenberg, PhD, established h2c, which represents glad organizations, solid individuals, the principal association to have practical experience in training pioneers on the workmanship and study of building upbeat, elite organizations. Her saying, saying that satisfaction rises to benefit, has become a backbone for both her own life and those she serves the world over. Appreciation is one of the most embraced qualities around the world. Appreciation is character quality and adds to life satisfaction and fulfillment. Appreciation suggests mindfulness and being grateful. Appreciation can be worked by focusing on positive perspectives. There are solid and approved exercise to construct appreciation, for example, journaling and composing organized appreciation letters. Studies and trials show a straightforwardly corresponding relationship amongst satisfaction and appreciation and a backhanded connection amongst appreciation and melancholy, which is in accordance with the definition and finding of gloom.

Appreciation or the statement of thankfulness for some other person or thing produces best outcomes if it is rehearsed day by day, in a genuine way. It is concurred by most methods of reasoning that appreciation is a fundamental manifestation of prudence and essential piece of health. More examinations show a straightforwardly relative connection among's confidence and appreciation. More research and instructing shows that appreciative people gain more and quicker ground towards individual objective accomplishments. People who score high in appreciation levels revealed more excitement and vitality than those people who score lower. Appreciative individuals are focused outwards or on helping other people or outside causes; in this way, they are socially very much situated. Appreciation brings out other positive Excellencies in individuals.

Generally speaking, positive clinicians and clinical positive therapists concede to the relationship among's appreciation and human thriving or wellbeing or wellbeing or prosperity. It is unequivocally guessed that appreciation additionally positively connects to positive feelings and amiability and more examinations are being led. Appreciation can be a positive feeling when favors occur and when esteemed advantage happen. Right now, is an ethical indoor regulator or check or indicator for results? It is intriguing to see that appreciation is given free, subsequently the word. Studies show that appreciation benefits the individual being thankful and the individual who gets the appreciation. More examinations on the inspirations of appreciation are being directed. The more youthful people are, the more they are going to profit by appreciation; that is the reason it is essential to advance appreciation at the most youthful age conceivable. Increasingly more research is demonstrating this finding.

Positive thinking is all over. It has entered the corporate and business world consistently. Satisfaction is the thing that encourages individuals to lead a bona fide life; it is the thing that can help live in the now as opposed to conceding to a future that never comes. To be upbeat right now, individuals need to surrender all desire for a superior past.

Supporters of the positive psychology development trust one can figure out how to be cheerful. Individuals will in general become in a split second adverse, before positive individuals, and this is the place numerous individuals fail to understand the situation. What's to come is to a great extent how one characterizes it. As Winston Churchill stated, hopeful people see openings in each disappointment. X-ray scanners show portions of the mind light up when individuals grin. The more individuals animate the glad piece of the cerebrum, the less the other dark side gets a look in consequently why jaunty individuals state that everything is extraordinary, the entire time. The brain tickers that individuals are feeling energy and produces glad synthetic concoctions just from the tone. If individuals write down what achievement implies for them on a specific day, being specific.

THE BENEFITS OF KNOWING OUR DARK SIDE

In psychology, one piece of our own being is known as the Shadow (considering Carl Jung's theories). This shadow is our dark drive, our "dark side", as they say, a covered bit of ourselves that we overall would lean toward not to show up, not even to ourselves. We may not think about this perspective, we may even be hesitant to stand up to it. Notwithstanding, it's more intelligent to understand our dark side to get the going with focal points.

- You can use your imaginativeness and innovative psyche to perceive the bit of excusal in yourself. Some Shadow asks about activities base on drawing, mapping the mind, etc. Causing relationship with our stylish side to can improve our relationship with that covered part in all of us.

- You can fix any relationship regarding continuously genuine self-evaluation and direct correspondence. Since specific associations are hurt by covered objections, the more we see that we stow away, the more we can fathom those associations that simply break or break for no good reason.

- You can see what you "foresee" onto others, which by then shapes a segment of our appraisals about others. We all in all will when all is said in done discover in others what we expect of ourselves. By then, as opposed to genuinely knowing each other, we make "hypotheses" about what the other, relies upon our opinion of ourselves. Naturally, we can will all in all think and ask, "What am I doing that is him?" This is an incredible request if you understand you are doing it and not using it to absurdly condemn one's exercises or musings.

- You can discard the fault and disrespect that go with our negative feelings and, clearly, our awful exercises. We can truly see why the Catholic demonstration of affirmation has a veritable psychological favored position. All over, we ought to go facing our dark main impetuses with our fight for opportunity.

- You can deactivate any negative feelings that even amazingly occur in normal every day presence. We need to manage the negative events and conditions that lamentably plague us.

- Finally, you can achieve certified self-affirmation, a fuller self-affirmation: what your character is and what you can be.

Emotional Domain - Abyss

If you have felt the abyss, it is inconsequential to delineate it, in light of the fact that there are no veritable words to depict it. It may be known to be a dark and significant recognize that seems to have no substance, or if nothing else it feels like that when you are there. Right when you see that you are feeling debilitated, hopeless and lost, you see a dark and clearly ceaseless abyss. Rely upon it, from time to time it's too difficult to even consider evening consider going out in solitude with "Abyss". You must have a way clearing guide for clearness or clarification to know where you are. It is possible to find your way through the Abyss.

You may remember the film "The Abyss." I review the bits of the film where this man was at the base of the ocean, and he was for all intents and purposes torpid at this moment. He used the help of others to help him with journey of this "abyss." I genuinely couldn't confer or get consequently. The gathering he went to the ocean with worked as a gathering to help him. He was a savvy and capable man with bleeding edge getting ready in his field. In any case, he allowed the assistance of group people to manage him and sometimes accepted him to a position where he could breathe in openly. Feelings actuated by events, conditions, getaways, wants, mixed up suspicions, loss of a companion or relative, etc. At times this can make somebody sink into the Abyss.

Exactly when we are there, we feel that nobody needs to consider it, that nobody is available and that it is incredibly improbable out. Regardless of the way that your mind and experience may uncover to you something different, the study of your body changes and there is a difficulty that incapacitates it. You may feel so destroyed that you can't find a good pace. People have different techniques for delineating these feelings. Exactly when you feel it, your cerebrum makes negative considerations and techniques for assaulting any hints of joy around you. With an innovative and creative mind, there is no certified end to the virtuoso stories made to acknowledge that you are absolutely alone. Words that have all the earmarks of being essential and liberal can cause greater torment in you.

Assortments in feelings look like a continuum wherein unhappiness, inconvenience, and assessment of hopelessness are of evolving degrees. Physical manifestations moreover go with these feelings.

If you experience the evil impacts of physical and excited torment because of difficulty, pity, feelings of powerlessness and wretchedness, make a point to go to your objective and let your gathering oversee you towards your joy, fulfillment and comfort. , You may need to search for the help of your essential consideration doctor or other approved capable.

These specialists are arranged and have the fundamental experience to assess their specific needs. A specialist can be an expert, examiner, spousal and family consultant or social worker. Your friends and family are in like manner part of your gathering. Recollect that you may not see that they are available considering the way that your acknowledgment can upset or make the dream that they couldn't mindless. They stress

Conditions are difficult with fiscal change along these lines a great deal of control at the present time. We are social animals who are regularly fortifying in our experiences. If you don't live your trademark state of agreement and joy, you may decide to vanquish the feelings that cause misery and trouble. Take an interest and let your universe help you through those that help you to recollect how brilliant you are.

The "abyss" is a mental trip, and the fear that develops relies upon lies. Steps for the going with:

1. Speak with somebody you know and have love and care for.
2. Guidance therapeutic administrations capable, as above, even by phone. Your

local list much of the time contains an overview of social protection providers and emergency numbers.

3. Leave yourself and care when you can't deal with.

4. Make an overview of the joys in your life. In case you can't check the joys, come back to number 1 above and start again with these methods.

5. Record your considerations and check whether they show you or not.

6. Ask a family member, buddy, or therapeutic administrations capable to help you with finding the words to change your negative musings into engaging clarifications.

Example: Alone. Nobody calls me. Nobody comes to see me. I am reliably there for myself and never left. I'm not by any means the only one I can call friends and family. I'm going to visit a family member or associates now. These are just a couple of contemplations. Try not to spare a moment to keep mentioning help from "Abyss" until you decide to change your suppositions yourself. You can without a lot of stretch find a completely different world that inspires you.

DECEPTION

The going with kind of mind control that will be investigated is deception. This mind control technique will have two or three likenesses' to control in the way those controllers will use a great deal of deception so as to locate a functional pace objective. This fragment will go into more bits of information concerning how deception functions, the methodologies related with it, and a piece of the examination that has been found.

What is Deception?

In any case is the definition about what deception is. Deception, alongside subterfuge, confusion, imagines, misleading, and beguilement, is a show used by the position to spread emotions in the subject about things that are contortions or which are basically almost the whole way feelings. Deception can consolidate a collection of things, for example, disguise, and spread, impedance, capable deception, presentation, and dissimulation. The director will have the decision to control the cerebrum of the subject considering the way that the subject will trust in them. The subject will recognize what the ace is communicating and may even be basing reachable plans and forming their reality dependent on the things that the expert has been letting them know.

On the off chance that the master is rehearsing the methodology of deception, the things they have been telling the subject will be counterfeit. Trust can without a considerable amount of a stretch be pummeled once the subject discovers, which is the clarification the ace must be gifted at the technique of deception and exceptional at getting something moving if they need to proceed with their subject.

Typically, deception will come up the degree that affiliations and it can incite sentiments of vulnerability and unfaithfulness between the two partners who are in the relationship. This is considering the way that deception hurts the rules of most affiliations and is in like way observed to impact the needs that go with that relationship. Considerable number people need to have the choice to have a real discussion with their embellishment; if they have discovered that their partner is surprising, they would need to understand how to use confusion and impedance to get the solid and reasonable data that they need. The trust would in like way be gone from the relationship, making it difficult to develop the relationship back to where it had once been. The subject would dependably be exploring the things that the ace was outlining for them, thinking about whether the story was authentic or something made up. Because of this new vulnerability, most affiliations will end once the subject finds a couple of arrangements concerning the deception of the master.

Sorts of Deception

Deception is a sort of correspondence that depends upon oversights and lies so as to persuade the subject of the world that best fits the ace. Since there is correspondence required, there will in like way be a few specific sorts of deception that could be happening. As appeared by the Interpersonal Deception Theory, there are 5 undeniable sorts of deception that are found. A piece of these have been appeared in different sorts of mind control, displaying that there can be some covering. The five basic sorts of deception include:

Deceptions: This is the place the overseer makes up data or gives data that is by no means equal to what is reality. They will demonstrate this data to the subject as truth and the subject will consider it to be reality. This can be risky since the subject won't grasp that they are being proceeded with sham data; if the subject comprehended the data was false, they would not likely be talking with the power and no deception would happen.

Avoidances: this is the place the head will make negating, crude, or degenerate clarifications. This is done to lead the subject to get disordered and to not get a handle on what's happening. It can correspondingly assist the head with disguising any trace of disappointment if the subject returns later and tries to reprimand them for the phony data.

Mask: This is one of the most for the most part saw sorts of deception that are used. Masks are the place the manager disregards data that is material or essential to the specific condition, deliberately, or they look into any immediate that would cover data that is fitting to the subject for that specific setting. The chairman won't have truly misdirected the subject; anyway they will have ensured that the basic data that is required never makes it to the subject.

Bending: this is the place the director will exaggerate a reality or distort a touch to turn the story the way wherein that they may require. While the authority may not be truly deceptive the subject, they are going to cause the circumstance to appear as though a more conspicuous strategy than it truly is or they may change reality a piece with the target that the subject will do what they need.

Under-depictions: a modest depiction of the truth is the exact opposite of the paltriness device in that the head will make light of or constrain bits of this present reality. They will tell the subject that an occasion isn't that goliath obviously of activity when in truth it could be what picks whether the subject finds the opportunity to graduate or gets that colossal progress. The ace will have the choice to return later and say how they didn't perceive how epic of a strategy it was, leaving them to look amazing and the subject to search in every way that really matters irrelevant on the off chance that they fight.

These are only a couple of the sorts of deception that may be found. The star of deception will use any procedure that is open to them to locate a useful pace objective, much like what happens in different sorts of mind control. If they can appear at their objective using another methodology against the subject, by then they will do it so the rundown above isn't the littlest piece specific. The chairman of deception can be staggeringly perilous because the subject won't have the choice to admit all with what is and what a demonstration of deception is; the star will be so talented at what they do that it will be essentially difficult to comprehend what is reality and what isn't.

Habits of thinking in Deception

Specialists have asserted that there are three essential objectives that are open in deceptions found in agreeable affiliations. These would unite frill focused points, pompous perspectives, and relationship focused habits of thinking.

We should take a gander at the embellishment focused desires first. At this moment technique for thinking, the manager will use deception so as to abstain from making hurt the subject, or their collaborator. They may in like way use the deception to ensure the subject's relationship with an outside outsider, to refuse having the subject stress over something, or to keep the assurance of the subject immaculate. A significant part of the time, this sort of inspiration for deception will be seen as socially important comparatively as socially mindful.

This sort of deception isn't as awful as a section of the others. On the off chance that the director gets some answers concerning something loathsome that the subject's closest companion said about them, the expert may close-lipped regarding it. While this is a sort of deception, it helps the subject keep that participation while protecting the subject from feeling frightful for themselves. This is the sort of deception that is discovered the most generally speaking seeing somebody and may in like way not cause that much harm whenever found. Most couples would use this sort of deception so as to ensure about their right hand.

Next is oneself focused way of thinking of deception. This one isn't viewed as respectable as the first and is right now looked slipping on than changed techniques. Rather than battling with the subject and how they are feeling, the executive is going to simply consider how they feel and about their own unique mental self portrayal. At the present time, chairman is using the deception so as to ensure about or improve their own psychological self view. This kind of deception is used so as to shield the star from assessment, mortification, or stun.

Right when this deception is used in the relationship, it is overall seen to be a more significant issue and offense than what is found with the frill focused deception. This is considering the way that the master is acting in a prejudiced manner as opposed to trying to ensure the relationship or the other right hand.

At last, the relationship focused technique for thinking of deception. This deception will be used by the chairman in the longing for keeping any shrewdness that may go to the relationship just by evading social injury and struggle. Subordinate upon the condition, this sort of deception will every now and then assistance the relationship and at different occasions it may be the clarification behind hurting the relationship since it will make things sensibly caught. For example, on the off chance that you cover how you are feeling about dinner since you would slant toward not to get in a battle, this may bolster the relationship. Then again, on the off chance that you busy with extramarital relations and close-lipped regarding this data, it is basically going to make things progressively confused at long last.

Notwithstanding the purpose of deception in the relationship, it isn't proposed. The ace is holding data that may be fundamental to the subject; when the subject finds a couple of arrangements concerning it, they will begin to lose trust in the ace and marvel what else the executive is escaping from them. The subject won't be unreasonably worried for the clarification for the deception, they will fundamentally be vexed that something has been kept from them and the relationship will start to have a section. It is once in a while best to stay with the arrangement of validity in the relationship and encircle yourself with people who don't rehearse deception in your social party.

Perceiving Deception

If the subject is enthused about maintaining a strategic distance from deception in their life so as to keep up a key decent ways from the mind games that go with it, it is as frequently as conceivable a sharp plan to understand how to recognize when deception is going on. Reliably, it is difficult for the subject to find that deception is going on except for if the master goofs and either lies that is clear or noticeable or they repudiate something that the subject undeniably knows to be genuine. While it might be difficult for the chairman to cheat the subject for an important stretch, it is something that will by and large happen in typical ordinary nearness between people who know one another. Recognizing when deception happens is regularly hazardous considering the path that there are less any pointers that are completely solid to tell when deception occurs.

Deception, in any case, is set up for setting an enormous load on the academic working of the manager since they ought to fathom how to review the greater part of the clarifications that they have made to the subject so the story stays conceivable and obvious. One oversight and the subject will have the decision to tell that something isn't right. Considering the strain of keeping the story straight, the head is by and large progressively slanted to opening out data to alert the subject either through nonverbal or verbal signs.

Examiners recognize that unmistakable deception is a system that is dynamic, liquid, and complex and which will routinely sway subordinate upon the message that is being traded. As showed by the Interpersonal Deception Theory, deception is an iterative and dynamic strategy for impact between the master, who attempts to control the data how they need it with the target that it isn't proportional to this present reality, and the subject, who will by then endeavor to comprehend if the message is certified or not. The master's activities will be interrelated to the moves that the subject makes after they get the message. During this trade, the master will uncover the nonverbal and verbal data that will signal the subject in to the deceptive. At certain focuses, the subject may have the decision to tell that the master has been misleading them.

Fundamental Components of Deception

While it might be difficult to comprehend which components show when deception is going on, there are a few sections that are customary of deception. Reliably the subject won't understand that these parts have happened except for if the director has lied or been trapped in the show of misdirecting. These are parts that will be seen later on if the director is using the arrangement of deception in the correct manner. The three principle bits of deception join cover, disguise, and reenactment.

Cover

The significant bit of deception is disguise. This is the place the director is trying to cover reality in another manner with the target that the subject won't appreciate that they are feeling the loss of the data. From time to time this strategy will be used when the chairman uses misleading explanations when they are telling data. The subject won't understand that the disguising has happened until later when these certainties are uncovered as it were. The ace will be gifted in covering reality with the target that it is staggeringly difficult for the subject to locate a couple of arrangements concerning the deception by some accidental occasion.

Disguise

Disguise is another part that can be found during the time spent deception. When this occurs, the administrator is endeavoring to establish a connection of being some other individual or thing. This is when the authority is hiding something imperative to them from the subject, for example, their certifiable name, what they achieve for an employment, who they have been with, and what they are up to when they go out. This goes more distant than basically changing the outfit that somebody wears in a play or a film; when disguise is used during the time spent deception, the administrator is endeavoring to change their whole persona in order to delude and deceive the subject.

There are a couple of examples that can outline the use of disguise during the time spent deception. The first is in a long time to the master covering themselves, generally as another person, so they are not indisputable. The administrator may do this in order to get by and by into a crowd of people that couldn't care less for them, change their characters to make somebody like them, or for another inspiration to propel their destinations. Once in a while, the word disguise can insinuate the administrator covering the certified thought of a suggestion with desires for hiding an effect or motivation that is detested with that recommendation. Every now and again this sort of disguise is found in proclamation or political turn.

Disguise can be hazardous because it is hiding the authentic thought of what's going on. In case the master is covering who they are from the subject, it might be very difficult for the subject to figure out who they genuinely are. When information is held from the subject, it fogs how they can think since they don't have the right information to choose reasonable choices. While the subject may feel that they are choosing astute choices readily, the master has expelled key information that may change the subject's point of view.

Reenactment

The third piece of deception is known as reenactment. This involves indicating the subject information which is counterfeit. There are three systems that can be used in reenactment including interference, production, and mimicry. In mimicry, or the recreating of another model, the pro will be unwittingly depicting something that resembles them. They may have an idea that resembles someone else's and instead of giving credit; they will say that it is all theirs. This kind of reenactment can much of the time occur through sound-related, visual, and different techniques.

Assembling is another device that the administrator may use when using deception.

This implies the administrator will take something that is found when in doubt and change it with the objective that it is exceptional.

They may describe to a story that didn't happen or incorporate embellishments that intensify it sound best or over it really was. While the focal point of the story may be legitimate, yes they got an awful assessment on a test, it will have some extra things put in, and for example, the educator gave them a terrible assessment purposely. In reality the administrator didn't contemplate and that is the explanation they got the horrible assessment regardless.

Finally, interference is another kind of amusement in deception. This is when the administrator endeavors to get the subject to focus on a choice that is other than the real world; generally by prodding or offering something that might be more luring than reality that is being covered up. For example, if the spouse is cheating and thinks the wife is starting to discover, he may bring home a valuable stone ring to redirect her from the issue for a brief time span. The issue with this framework is that it every now and again doesn't prop up long and the master must discover another way to deal with mislead the subject in order to prop the methodology up.

Research on Deception

Deception has become a significant bit of ordinary everyday presence. Whether or not the authority plans to cause hurt or not, there are various events where deception will sneak in to associations of different sorts. The administrator may deceive their director in order to get greater chance to finish an endeavor; a spouse may mislead their accessory in order to not outrage them. While various cases are not to cause harmed, they are so far present in society. Because of this inescapability, there has been asking about done to endeavor to choose why it occurs and who may undoubtedly play out the exhibits.

Social Research

Socially there has been some investigation done to see the effects of deception on society. There are a couple of ways of thinking found in social research, for example, in psychology, which oversee deception. In these techniques, the investigators are going to intentionally mislead or trick their individuals with respect to what is really going on in the examination. This keeps the subjects ignorant concerning what's going on and will help with passing on better results.

An examination that was done in 1963 by Stanley Milgram shows how deception will tackle people. The masters told the subjects that they would aid an investigation that oversaw learning and memory; really this examination perceived how willing the subjects were to obeying requests of somebody who is in control, in any occasion, when that obeying inferred that they would need to apportion perpetual stock of different subjects. While the person who was getting the anguish was just an on-screen character and didn't for the most part get injured in the preliminary, it was discovered that the subjects would cause the most raised open torment on the performer whenever encouraged to do accordingly by the position. Close to the completion of this investigation, the subjects were resolved what the examination's genuine nature was and people were given assistance with solicitation to shield they left in a state of flourishing.

The use of deception right currently raised a lot of issues with investigate ethics. Starting at now it is being controlled by the American Psychological Association and other master bodies to ensure that the subjects are being managed tolerably and are not tolerating fix harmed at the same time.

Psychological Research

Psychological research is the branch that will use deception the most because this is basic to pick the outcomes that would genuinely occur. The methodology for thinking behind doing this deception imparts that people are delicate to the way wherein that they may appear to other people, correspondingly as to themselves, and the reluctance that they feel may bend or meddle with the way where the subject would act in standard conditions outside of doing the appraisal where they would not feel analyzed. The deception is intended to cause the subjects to feel calmer with the target that the genius can get intelligently precise outcomes.

For example, the genius may be intrigued to discover what conditions may cause an understudy to undermine a test. If the master asks the understudy absolutely, it isn't likely that the subjects would confess to bewildering and there would be zero opportunity to get for the head to comprehend who is coming clean and who isn't. For this situation, the master would need to use obstruction so as to get a cautious thought of how reliably dumbfounding happens.

The manager may rather say the assessment is to discover how normal the subject is; the subject may even be told during the technique that they may get the chance to see another person's answers before they give their own. Near the consummation of this evaluation that joins deception, it is necessitated that the ace notices to the subject what the real idea of the assessment is and why the deception was fundamental. Likewise, most overseers will besides give a quick outline of the outcomes that happened between the majorities of the people when the evaluation is all around done.

Despite how deception is used a great deal in these sorts of research thinks about, they are bound by the moral gauges set out by the American Psychological Association; there are a few discussions about whether deception is something that ought to be allowed using any methods. Some recognize that permitting deception isn't fundamental and it is making hurt the subjects who are sharing. Others recognize that the outcomes would be slanted if the subjects knew the away from of the appraisal early. Regularly the best issue with using deception in an assessment isn't only the certified deception. Or of course maybe, it is the disastrous treatment that is used in an assessment of this sort, comparatively as the repercussions of what will occur in the appraisal that is shocking. This is ordinarily the hidden motivation driving why some are against using these sorts of studies and why it is viewed as exploitative in nature.

Another contention against the morals of using deception in these sorts of studies is that the subject has as of late given their educated agree to look at the appraisal. They have been perused the rules and rules that go with the assessment and feel like they are shown enough the last things that are required to sign a waiver so as to start. It is fought that if the director is overpowering the subject and dismissing significant data about the assessment, offering little gratefulness to if it is to the best good situation of the evaluation, by then the subject really isn't instructed in any case. Along these lines, the subject ought not to be taking interests in the appraisal since they didn't unequivocally offer agree to the certifiable assessment being composed.

Despite the contentions that are out there on this theme, there have been some fascinating discoveries when the subjects are cheated about the possibility of the evaluation. For example, concerning the assessment referenced above about deceiving; if the subjects had been told about the real idea of the evaluation it isn't likely that by a long shot the majority of them would have cheated. This would be considering the way that none of them ought to be viewed as misleading or counterfeit to others around them.

The deception engaged the scientists to perceive what may occur in a certifiable application. So also, if the subjects of the memory test referenced before in the manual knew the veritable nature about that overview, they would not have been as in danger to look at the power figure and control the results that they did.

Regardless of the battles that have been encompassed about using deception in examine; the utilization of deception has furnished specialists with a colossal measure of fascinating outcomes. These outcomes most likely won't have been conceivable without the use of deception since the subject may have responded in a substitute manner to the evaluation.

Thinking

Psychology might be the standard clarification that deception is used in get some information about, yet there is additionally a great deal of deception that has appeared ok now. Taking everything into account, deception is an extraordinarily regular event in thinking. For example, in the assessments of Descartes that were passed on in 1641, the possibility of Deus deceptor was presented; this idea was something that had the decision to cheat the sentiment of self, when it was thinking dependably, about what was happening honestly. This idea kept on being used as a section of his hyperbolic helplessness; this is to recognize the subject by then starts to address everything that is available to address since they have been misled beforehand. A significant part of the time, suspicious clashes will use this Deus deceptor as their spine to place into helplessness or question the learning of reality that one individual holds. The fundamental piece of the contest imparts that everything the subject knows most likely won't be legitimately since it is unquestionably not difficult to sell out the subject.

This is only one of the events of deception found in thinking. Different works have been shaped on this theme trying to clarify precisely what it is, the way wherein it impacts the subject, and ways that the subject may have the choice to abstain from teaming up with it. There has besides been a colossal measure of research done trying to pick when deception might be fine and when it will all in all be unsafe. This is okay with stunning discussion; a few people recognize that all deception is appalling while others consider deception to be spare somebody's feelings as fine from time to time, for example, a spouse holding the way that somebody said something mean concerning their cherished one.

BODY LANGUAGE

Body language is the language you express without words. When you state, "correspondence" you frequently consider "words", "speeches", and "introductions". In any case, correspondence is considerably more than words. You can impart incredibly precisely without saying single word just with your body. All aspects of your body can talk as expressively as words; maybe, far and away superior to words.

The manner in which you stand, the manner in which you hold your head, the manner in which you position your palms, hands, arms, legs – everything says something. Some of the time, you can get the implied message in a moment – like when somebody is forceful – and here and there it requires some investment.

There are numerous hypotheses about how much correspondence we really do through body language. One that you will discover cited regularly is the Mehrabian hypothesis – by Dr Albert Mehrabian - which expresses that around 7 percent of correspondence is done through words, 38 percent is through the tone of our voice and an incredible 55 percent however body language. As it were, the non-verbal correspondence adds up to a surprising 93 percent.

Why is Body Language Important?

You would express something that add up to 93 percent is significant. This number itself – regardless of whether many state it surmised

– is tremendously amazing. This shows that it is so essential to figure out how to peruse body language – because the real message originates from that point. It is without a doubt imperative to realize what the other individual truly needs to pass on. This sort of data would make your life very simple.

A great many people can "get the signs" regardless of whether they don't really have the foggiest idea how to peruse body language. For instance, you go into a room and you "know" regardless of whether they were talking something agreeable or contending about something. The body language of the individuals in the room will "advise" you the temperament quickly, however if you were inquired as to why you concluded that you'd not have the option to clarify.

Figuring out how to precisely peruse body language is an expertise like some other, we as a whole love Sherlock Holmes and his stunning perception abilities. Analysts, FBI operators, individuals working in insight and secret activities, proficient speculators, performers, and such, are prepared in the craft of perusing body language. They use this ability to trick you into accepting that they are what-they-are-definitely not.

There are numerous signs that your body will send automatically. For instance, you'll frown at seeing regurgitation or defecation on a plate; you may grin at the image of a little cat playing or blossom sprouting or vehicle or pony dashing with forsake. Recognizing what these signs are would assist you with controlling correspondence so you could "transmit" the message you need transmitted.

Knowing to peruse body language would support you:

- Establish administration and keep up it disregarding rivalry;

- Establish a benevolent and helpful condition officially and casually any place you go;

- Amplify and advance your influence powers and along these lines having the option to get individuals do what you need them to do;

- Win individuals' trust;

- Ensure that you pick companions, associates, workers, and so on better.

These are just a bunch benefits you may pick up from figuring out how to peruse body language. The best is that you would have the option to remain in charge of most circumstances because you would know not exclusively to peruse others' signs yet in addition recognize what signals you ought to send when and where. Sounds like an idiot proof formula for progress!

Perusing Body Language Is All In Context

You definitely know to prepare body language, regardless of whether you may not realize that you know. A few models:

- You know when your manager strolls feeling foul even before he says single word;

- you realize your spouse is stressed over something regardless of whether he/she acts like nothing occurred;

- you realize your kid is concealing something with no genuine explanation at all;

- you know when your sweetheart is cheating without a smidgen of evidence;

- you realize that somebody is going to give you uplifting news or terrible news before they even opened their mouth;

- you realize that somebody is ready for a battle regardless of whether that individual never tended to you in any way;

- You realize that somebody detests you without them saying it words, etc.

This "you know" is you perusing body language automatically. Medically introverted individuals can't peruse body language; they just downplay and procedure words – subsequently, it is anything but difficult to "cheat" them because they process just what is imparted through words.

A great many people know to peruse what others pass on through their body language. Nonetheless, that won't help you to an extreme. Just when you figure out how to identify the better signals passed on and decipher it intentionally you would have the option to profit completely from this information. This is because when you arrive at that level, you never again marvel or uncertainty what you see; you know without a doubt and that information would place you in a profitable position. It's practically similar to you can guess what that person might be thinking.

Individual Telltale Body Language

You would think that it's simple to "comprehend" individuals whom you see regularly – your family, partners, companions, and so on. Each individual has an obvious sign for satisfaction, excitement, outrage, aggravation, lying, etc. For instance, you will realize that:

- When your manager begins drumming his fingers on the table, he is going to blast into a surge of abuse;

- when your spouse contacts her lower lip she is explicitly energized;

- When your spouse answers you while staying away from to take a gander at you, she is forceful irritated about what you're stating or doing, etc.

Base lining: How Do You Do It

After some time, it would turn out to be simple for you to peruse the nonverbal signs from the individuals you know. How would you read others; individuals whom you never met in your life? In math, when you have to include two parts with different denominator, you initially get the two portions to a shared factor. Thus, before you even endeavor perusing the individual/people, you have to pattern them first; get them to a shared factor, a base.

This would imply that you ought to have the option to take around 3-5 minutes to watch the individual/people to see how they act regularly. The elements that will enable you "to peruse" the individual accurately are, among others:

- The in general stance – is the individual slumping or standing straight with shoulders squared?

- The sitting style – are the legs crossed or are the feet kept grounded on the floor?

- The style of intersection – if the legs are crossed, would they say they are crossed to frame the figure four (one leg high on the thigh of the other), crossed at the lower leg or crossed at the knee?

- The standing style – is the individual remaining with feet together or wide separated?

- The motioning style – are hand motions moving outside the body's edge or are the signals contained inside a little circle? Are the motions striking and vivified? It is safe to say that they are refined or obtrusive?

- The tone of the voice delicate and curbed, or in line with the general voice of the room?

- Is the individual talking quick or the words accompanying a deliberate pace?

- Is the individual listening more or talking more?

- Does the individual look, or keeps eyes turned away or down?

Likewise observe how the individual deals with his helpless regions, for example the neck territory, the tummy button region and the crotch zone. If the hands are drifting near, the individual is at any rate awkward and at the most dreadful, on edge. If the individual keeps these territories uncovered and open, the message is that he is confident and confident.

You will realize the individual is available to the thought/people/place if:

- He permits the powerless regions of his body to be uncovered and open;

- He remains with feed wide separated taking more space than required;

- He keeps his hands on the hip or at the sides open and free;

- He sits folding his legs to frame figure-4.

You will realize he is bound to be non-responsive, antagonistic or not intrigued if:

- Hands are drifting to cover the powerless regions;

- The arms are collapsed over the chest;

- Legs are firmly crossed like interlaced;

- Stands with legs contacting or extremely near one another;

- One arm getting the other, which is at the side of the body.

When you gauge an individual, you would have the option to peruse his body language better, because it would be in setting. The adjustment in body language would the non-verbal reaction to your correspondence. Non-verbal correspondence would help unravel what really the other individual needs. What are the signs saying?

Notice the changes.

- Is the individual the equivalent while conversing with you as he when he was moving alone (unwatched)?

- Is he grinning less or more? Is the grin authentic or counterfeit?

- Are the hands uneasy? Did they vanish into the pockets? Do they make rough motions?

- Are they happy with standing close or they moving away?

- Do the shoulders descend or settle or would they say they are unbending?

- Does the voice get stronger or gentler?

- Is the tone well disposed, chilly, compromising, and welcoming?

Check how the verbal and nonverbal signs match to each other.

- Repeats what the words state. For instance, the sentence, "I'm eager" would be joined by the hand moving to the stomach tapping it. This implies the individual is coming clean with 100%.

- Contradicts what the words are stating. For instance, saying "I love you" while the eyes look at all other ladies in the room.

- Substitutes non-verbal finishes paperwork for words. For instance, eyes exhausted or loaded up with appall say substantially more than words can say.

- Complement the words. For instance, the manager applauding a representative while handling a gesture of congratulations.

- Accenting the words. For instance, saying boisterously, "I deviate" and simultaneously slamming your clench hand against the table before you.

It is extremely difficult to counterfeit non-verbal language. Your body consequently responds to the musings that experience your psyche and that response isn't automatic, yet additionally crude. It frequently resists control. When you endeavor to control it, you really turn out as phony.

Realize what signs to search for to accomplish your own objective.

- You need to know whether the individual is tuning in to you with intrigue? The signs that will affirm this is immediate eye to eye connection, body inclining towards you, body's position is open and the arms and legs are loose.

- You need to know if somebody is pulled in to you. Watch for prolonger eye to eye connection, comforting grin, closer to you standing, slight however warm and welcoming touch, head and body inclining towards you.

- You need to know whether the individual is lying or coming clean. Hope to signs, for example, uneasy hands, contacting face (nose and mouth region), shooting eye contact, increasing squinting or unblinking look.

Basic Idioms on Body Language Translated

The importance of body language is progressively regular that you'd think. Numerous articulations and sayings we use in our everyday discoursed have further implications that allude to body language. Here are a couple of models:

Investigate my eyes and state, ***"This isn't valid"***

This depends on the way that an individual who is lying would not have the option to look at an individual without flinching. Consequently, when you tell somebody, "Investigate my eyes and state it", you are alluding to this reason.

In any case, as you would find in the parts that follow, this reason isn't in every case genuine – particularly when seen in confinement. To be certain that the individual who isn't "investigating your eyes" isn't lying you have to take a gander at in setting. Now and then, looking to a great extent isn't because the individual needs to stay away from your look, but since they are thinking or examining data.

Pay close attention to me

You express words with your lips. This is clear and genuine. Be that as it may, your lips can talk without expressing a word also. Bended upwards it shows satisfaction, bended down trouble, gnawing lips apprehension, twist one side snigger, straight line upsetting, etc. You know when you watch the lips what the individual may be thinking – acceptable terrible, ill bred, testing, upbeat, tragic, irate, and so forth.

Henceforth, "read my lips" really caused to notice what isn't stated, for example the non-verbal signal. Seeing what people do with their lips is an incredible method to pick up understanding into what they are thinking and plan to do.

Converse with my hand

There are numerous motions that are expressive to the point that words could get unessential. In any case, hand motions dissimilar to general facial motions can mean different things in different nations. It is in this way significant that you don't use hand motion in an outside nation except if you are 100 percent sure that you comprehend what it really implies there.

These feet were intended for strolling

This resembles an easy decision. Obviously, feet are intended for strolling. Be that as it may, feet are articulate speakers too. They do demonstrate a craving "to leave" – and this in the setting would show lack of engagement, fervor, dread, etc.

For instance, young lady's feet when pointed inwards state that she would prefer to be without anyone else; she isn't happy. A sales rep's feet, if moving, would imply that he is energized that he is going to get it done/make a deal. If two people are talking and one of them has his chest area inclining towards the other, however feet pointing outward it implies that he needs to leave.

Isn't it intriguing how expressively can the feet talk?

Establish a first connection

The manner in which an individual sees you just because imprints itself on the brain and the body's response will for quite a while react to that picture of you. This is the reason it is critical to make that "early introduction" a great one.

This implies your entire body communicates in a similar language.

For instance, you are going for a meeting for a center administration or section level position. They are searching for a trustworthy, grounded individual with strong foundation in promoting. You show up with a faultless scholastic reputation, great experience talk extraordinary – however have a mariner's tattoo on your neck, a hoop and brushed your hair like a mafia wear. Do you think you'll get the activity?

Let us take a gander at another scene. You're arranging a serious deal for your organization and you need to go over confident and trustworthy. You give a limp and sweat-soaked handshake, your hands aren't at present for one minute and your eyes are dashing back and forth the room. Do you think you are motivating the organization's agent with trust and certainty?

It is significant that you recognize what your body is stating, the same amount of you realize how to peruse what the other individual's body is stating. Communication, all things considered, is a two-way street.

Body Language Myths You Should Know About

Not generally the body language signals are discernible as given in the book. Here and there – truth be told, the majority of the occasions – you have to focus on the setting to the ready to peruse precisely what you see. Additionally, there are myths that proliferate around body language that could lose you truly awful. It is significant that you know about a portion of these frequently experienced myths so you don't wind up in cumbersome or even risky circumstance because you misread the signs.

Myth 1: No Eye Contact Means Lying

Truth: Not really. Essentially, not meeting the eyes implies the individual isn't happy with what he is doing or saying. There could be 1001 reasons why the individual isn't happy – other than lying. Then again, a rehearsed liar would really meet your eyes square on and disclose to you a lie without squinting. Might shift the eyes after he lied; however one can lie while looking at you straight without flinching.

Subsequently, not all the people who can't look at you without flinching are lying; as not all people who look at you without flinching, are not coming clean with you. You have to search for a blend of other indications to mention an exact objective fact.

It is advantageous to make reference to here that the vast majority process data with the assistance of their sentiments, hearing and sight. Subsequently, if they are picturing it they will turn upward; if they need to hear it, they will look from side to side; if they are feeling it, they would look down on all fours. Looking into, sides to side or to the hands – all imply that a procedure of thinking/judging is occurring. This is certainly way off the mark to lying.

Myth 2: Crossing Arms Means "Not Interested"

Truth: While the facts demonstrate that people would ordinarily fold their arms when they need to put an obstruction among something and themselves, it doesn't constantly imply that. Some of the time, it's excessively cold and you fold your arms. At times, that is the most agreeable position – for instance, when the seat doesn't have arm rest. Here and there, crossing arms implies the individual is thinking something inside and out and with incredible focus.

You have to look past the stance much of the time, to get the genuine picture. Check the setting before you make any inferences. Then again, abstain from folding your arms over your chest while you are meeting new people in case you'll be perused as uninterested or unfriendly.

Myth 3: Fidgety People Are Perhaps Hiding Something

Truth: The normal conviction is that concealing something makes an individual awkward and subsequently, the individual seems to be uneasy. By and by, you have to take a gander at this perspective in setting. Assume the individual is confronting a significant meeting, introduction, or any such occasion which is of basic significance, it is typical for an individual to be somewhat apprehensive. It is apprehension that makes people squirm. If the circumstance is upsetting, some level of restlessness is adequate.

Myth 4: Anyone Who Talks Fast Is Conning You

Truth: People who are nervous may some of the time talk quick. People who are overenthusiastic about something will talk quick. Additionally people who are on edge to persuade you about something they feel is either essential to you or to them, will talk quick. In conclusion, at times people talk quick because that is the manner in which they talk.

Before you make your inferences, guarantee that you comprehend the foundation. It is in every case great to search for other indications before concluding that the individual who talk's quick isn't to be trusted.

Myth 5: A Good Verbal Communication Will Compensate For Deficient Body Language

This is regularly the thought with people who make introductions or require giving talks. In all actuality anyway solid and steady you are words are rarely enough. Over 30 minutes two people can trade around 800 non-verbal signs. Do you despite everything figure you don't have to get ready for the non-verbal side of the discussion?

OVERCOME ANGER AND AGGRESSION.

Anger is a feeling centered around control.

Somebody considers you a "moron dolt" and you feel furious. Somebody stops before you out on the town and you feel angered. Somebody assaults your amigo and you feel enraged. Somebody discloses to you that you won't get the remuneration increment you think you authenticity and feel irate. What disturbs you? What are these conditions in like manner?

Anger is acknowledged by the loss of control over components that sway fundamental qualities. The qualities that appeared in the past models can be pride, common sense, the individual you love, cash or a "reasonable" work; We are confused that we are not getting what we require or imagine.

In anger, we when in doubt may assume we comprehend what caused the issue. We have objectives for our anger. It may be the individual who denounces you, the individual who sets you off the street, the assailant, your chief or even you yourself. With anger, we can expect an effect of vitality made against the hazard out of vanquishing him. Or on the other hand, we can anticipate that an effect of importance ought to disconnect the breaking point that shields us from appearing at our objective.

Anger can every once in a while be used significantly. This can give us the vitality we have to battle if we are truly trapped. In any case, when in question, this reasonable darkens our judgment and makes extra weight. In the event that anger causes extraordinary direct toward others, it can everlastingly hurt affiliations, particularly those we love. Conceded or customary anger (smooth anger) has shown to be a basic clarification behind cardiovascular issues and respiratory dissatisfactions. This is the criminal behind "Type A" lead.

Restricting vibe recommends not suffering steady nature

What is the goings with examples of restricting vibe in like manner? Challenge to the cop to reprimand you. Pound on a decimated entryway. Censure every one for your issues for how your people raised you. Refusal to perceive that the relationship is over the top when this is clearly the situation. Start focusing on subsequent to losing the game. Continue hitting after you become familiar with the movement.

Notwithstanding the way that anger can every so often be ruinous, it isn't as awful as a threatening vibe. Mr. George Kelly felt that the essential driver of any undermining vibe was not the best attestation of the enduring bits of this current reality. An undermining vibe surmises not suffering reality. The unfriendly vibe is the upkeep of an objective significantly after undeniably it can't be developed. The threatening vibe is associated with accomplishing something "anxious" for something, paying little heed to the real world. Ill-disposed vibe harms you, you and others. The standard sound response to truth of a "perceived the reality of the situation" is to remember it and try to get it. Cautious Dr. Maslow perceived life's hardships and deficiencies by bearing that the water was wet.

If you should be upbeat and have taken in the techniques depicted at the present time, recognize you can be vivacious later on, paying little notice to the real world. So handle this past, pardon, let go, and proceed ahead.

Acknowledge responsibility for emotions and inventive contemplations about anger.

Anger is accomplished by your delicacy to modify sensibly to express conditions. On the off chance that you have a consistent anger issue, you have vital fundamental issues that you have not yet lit up, or you are using vivacious modifying systems that are not mind blowing.

There are different interior and outside techniques for administering anger. Different frameworks that help with any negative feelings also help with anger. Loss of saw control to accomplish regard for basic qualities causes anger. To defeat your anger, it is useful to see these imperative attributes and comprehend why you may require trust in your own capacity to be perky.

Accusing others (or yourself) and being angry may appear as though the path of least resistance. Discovering better approaches to manage consider the condition and fulfill you require a great deal of exertion. If you need to decrease your anger, consider the going with issues or structures to recover mental control.

1. Look at the estimations of torment and dread that underlie anger.

Recall that anger begins from dread and presumptions of inadequacy. An essential worth or objective is undermined and you believe you are losing control of the circumstance. You most likely won't have any desire to confess to being harmed or frightened. (You may imagine that such a certification implies, that shortcoming). In any case, focal evaluations will help you in recognizing the qualities and focuses on that are being alluded to.

The certifiable hazard may not be a shallow issue (late film) and a chief issue (it doesn't have any sort of impact to somebody you treasure or have been battered). Different sentiments of dread and torment will open the entrance to these fundamental issues. When you are in contact with dread and enduring, what are the covered pictures, considerations, and issues identified with them?

2. Build up a mindful appreciation.

My explicitly hurting customer has discovered that stirring up a continuously significant and compassionate valuation for a dad and thinking about him is unequivocally one of the keys to spreading his anger.

If you choose to reduce your anger against somebody, the hidden development is to do everything conceivable to see the condition from your perspective. As an issue of first significance, you can request to clarify your position. Urge them to take a gander at basic suspicions, emotions, or authentic parts that may have driven them to get their position or direct. Consolidate what they state and their notions from the viewpoint (so they similarly can comprehend their perspective). Understanding your condition, your perspective, and the reason behind your emotions and direct is commonly a basic avoidance to controlling anger.

To excuse isn't to disregard, to recall and to enjoy.

If it's difficult to have this kind of discussion with somebody, attempt to envision an understanding situation that enables you to quiet your anger. Considering my consideration with people in equivalent conditions, I attempt to envision what they may think and why.

On the off chance that you don't have the foggiest idea with respect to the individual all around okay to know your viewpoints, what may you have the choice to do? Remind the customer that he is so irate in the wake of being assaulted by a man that he will never watch him again. We test our assessment of human instinct. Alright have the alternative to perceive human limit as it truly may be? Alright have the alternative to see the way that there are pack killings, pre-adult abuse, and theft of my property, indiscreet lead or some different dangerous occasion without detonating? Alright have the choice to perceive that a few people advantage by me and "get out"? So as to control our anger paying little mind to hopeless occasions, we all must understand how to manage the "dark side" of life. Issues of selling out, bad form and rights are talked about.

3. Foresee best destinations (at any rate much as could reasonably be ordinary)

As Mike recognized his significant other's clarifications behind being late ought to have harmed him, the anger expanded. On the off chance that she demands bits of knowledge, for example, "He couldn't contemplate me," "She is careless," "I won't do this to her," or "She is so prideful," she will anger her.

Or then again perhaps, you can disentangle your fundamental wants as a genuine need to oversee yourself. You can concentrate more on the verification of the over a critical time length that you love him and make the fundamental strides not to hurt him. The way where you think enlarges or decreases your anger. Try to recognize that people's best destinations until you emphasize the signs that they seem to have changed desires.

As a clinician who has seen various customers, I have discovered that even the most ill-disposed people don't by and large undertaking to hurt others. Or then again perhaps, they need to ensure about themselves or others and regard their own qualities. (The most bargaining people are a significant part of the time people who have been mishaps of abuse and examination and are particularly delicate to them.) This thought dissipates by a wide margin a large portion of my anger.

This thought doesn't for the most part propose that I will quit using the results to hose trading off behavior. Regardless, that induces they can treat the individual fundamentally more noteworthy quietness and enough.

How to apply the discernment that people are inclined to being convincing so as to shield themselves against less threatening people? If the individual who by and large considers you is angered or intentionally harms you, they obviously do it for secure or esteem. He likely figures you accomplished something first, quiet down, or attempt to "give yourself a few things" to quit harming him. To spread it out basically, it obviously works for undefined reasons from it does in rehashing a question cycle! It gets a handle on your most exceedingly terrible wants, regardless of whether you don't stress over it or intentionally hurt it.

4. Are "capital" or "right" an issue with no reason?

Our needs are reliably the way in to our feelings. We can't perceive that others are defective or blemished. "Appalling", "awful", "exploitative" things happen billions of times each day. It is totally expected to feel negative slants, for example, anger considering occasions we call "unpleasant" or "beguiling."

The statute of "balance" versus "elation." The rule of value says that "life should dependably be reasonable and unquestionably the equivalent for everybody." If we have such a huge number of needs subject to this "training of praiseworthy nature," we are bound to the nearness of wretchedness. In a perfect world, people spend a considerable measure of their lives checking capital, offsetting what they got with what they gave, and keeping up the sort of bookkeeping framework they made. - That is completely settled on considerations of correspondence. This game-plan of sentiments in the capital may maybe have little correspondence with outside this current reality.

What is "right" for specific people who are ordinarily familiar with carefree and prosperous families and live fruitful, long and enthusiastic lives, while others are typically familiar with miserable conditions and pass on vigorous in the wake of driving a nearness of torment? "Bad form" wraps us. I suggest surrendering the "show of reliability".

It may be supplanted by the demonstration of satisfaction. He reports that I will pick the one that contributes most to my joy and the joy of others. I perceive that my life and the entirety of my choices is a gift. If I differentiate my gifts and those of others, particularly the people who have more, I will essentially diminish the valuation for my own one of kind blessings.

There is truly "esteem" at the present time. The thing I said about "esteem" is that requesting adherence to the examination of significant worth can undermine our joy. In any case, one of the anxieties people let me know is that in the event that they don't hold brisk to this standard, there will be no worth or result.

I request that people audit that we live in a world obliged by run of the mill laws that we can't "break". Trademark laws give some degree of standard outcomes: prizes and teaches for our activities. The affiliation can in like way make laws that give extra prizes and trains. The at risk social occasions as regularly as conceivable appear to go unpunished. In what limit may we control our anger when we see such a legitimate mistake?

"Mental Justice." Psychological laws are particularly productive as a trademark discipline. People who advantage by others are repulsed for trademark responses, for example, the nonattendance of certifiable closeness and love in their lives. They are repulsed for their Higher Self, who sees "harmfulness" or fiendishness to other people and passes on oblige over common empathy for others. They are repulsed for their anger and negative sentiments that plague them with fight, anger, and anxiety. They are too included to even consider evening consider evening consider getting frustrated to feel glad.

For example, Stalin and Hitler are two men who can share the qualification that has made more damage man than some other man ever. Some said these people were examples of how a harmful power could pay, as though to appear there was no worth. In any case, when the two perceived phenomenal riches and mind blowing normal effect, they proceeded with an ambush life. Perceiving that it is so difficult to be joyful for upbeat people makes me surrender a piece of my anger when something appears "misguided".

Handle reality and reason. Some piece of our anger may start from the conviction that others have gotten strangely more from us. We can accuse people who have more cash, significance, achievement or joy, particularly on the off chance that we don't recognize they merit it. We may imagine that life has acquainted with us a "disaster" if we look for after the "instructing of value." How may we have the alternative to smash anger at somebody who has something they "don't justify"? The resolution of significant worth says that people ought to just get what they merit.

The investigation of joy says that to be fun loving, we should perceive that things don't generally have all the reserves of being correct. I accept that the other individual and I can comprehend how to be content with what we have been given, regardless of whether it isn't by and large "equal" or "reasonable." Who knows what legitimate impacts of their "benefits" may be? Different poverty stricken people are more joyful than different rich people. What show will assist you with bettering control of your anger and feel dynamically joyful?

We perceived how my ambush customer could dispose of his significant anger with thankfulness and absolving. Comprehension and clearing are the pivotal components for any equation to diminish anger.

We can comparably battle to exculpate ourselves. We may be angered with ourselves since we are up 'till now living with the aftereffects of the ghastly choices we made before for the term of normal everyday presence. We may think we are so "repulsive" or "imbecile" that we don't save the choice to be lively. In what limit may we pardon ourselves for pounding our lives? We can impugn our people or even "God" for making us as people who "fizzled." It might shout out the imprint. In what limit may we accuse ourselves or others of our mishaps?

The equity principle says that we should get exactly what we "merit." The "capital show" implies that the people who have more than "their advantages" should be ousted from the stipend, while the people who have shy of what they "merit" should get more. This standard says that we should perhaps be sprightly when all records are balanced. Up to that point, we have to spend our lives improving equality, and that will never happen.

The show of fulfillment says: 1-Forget reasonable accounting; 2 recognize life as it is by and by; 3 unequivocally loving ourselves just as others - making our delight (and the joy of others) a basic goal; and as requirements be 4 exercises. Denouncing ourselves or others, fault, stress, accounting, scorn, and different futile negative thoughts are just a tangle agreeable to us.

[Note: Accepting the instructing of fortune doesn't infer that we won't be firm in actualizing contracts or various concurrences with others. We can combine prizes and disciplines into understandings and take measures to compensate and repel others to rouse them as required. This isn't identical to executing a "value" or "revenge" contract.]

5. Is it genuine that you are "trapped" on anger (or torment) for motivation?

"Do you keep your anger out" or feel you have been hurt to repel the person? Okay prefer to rebuke a person with "requital" (considering the "guideline of fairness")? You may have the choice to begin to see how the "respectability educating" isn't working outstandingly. You may accept that you should repel them by ending their anger. Gripping anger or torment can simply harm you!

In case you will probably change one's direct, you can use prizes and disciplines to affect lead. Nevertheless, don't adjust to the outcomes of feeling requital or anger. Does this with compassion as a way to deal with empower them to learn? Hold on for it to hush up. Tranquilly communicating your reasons is fundamentally more convincing than rebuking anger! (A significant part of the time, repay is more convincing than discipline.)

PRACTICE: Make a dissent list. Make a "fight list" for yourself just as others. Try superseding the "guideline of respectability" with the "educating of fortune" to deal with the issues that underlie any "mistake." Empathize with the other individual, recognize reality, and focus on streamlining fulfillment for the future for each huge thing on the once-over.

6. Dissect basic wants.

Unfulfilled wants can incite anger. What are your wants for yourself just as others right now? Do you foresee more than is pragmatic for this person right now?

Test your fundamental suspicions in regards to what you ought to be happy and continue with the presence you need. Test your wants for others. It may have higher (or special) standards than the others. You can foresee that others should tail them basically like you. You can even be right. In any case, these are your wants for others, not theirs. They are as they appear to be, and one of the basic establishments of anger isn't enduring people (or events) as they might be.

The "considering rights" and the select models of what we should get motivate the tendency that we are "tied." Some consider themselves to be misused individuals and view the world unfavorably. These wants are at the establishment of a significant sentiment of shortcoming and long stretch scorn at "off the mark" treatment. They are the most significant wellspring of anger for certain people.

7. Pick joy as opposed to anger: "Anger hurts me more than hurt."

Keeping up anger has different trivial outcomes. These results fuse negative effects on your body and cripple your satisfaction with respect to the present moment. You can't be angry and peppy at the same time, it's amazing! So you have a choice: anger or fulfillment!

People who generally pick anger over joy lead a disillusioned and incensed life, yet not rapture. Remember these results to all the more probable control your anger. State to yourself, "Why pick anger when I can consider thoughts that produce joy?" Use these 8 systems for anger control. See also other unbelievable frameworks in the book, especially the six character control methods that work agreeably (CHUG-OF: choice, agreeableness, getting, targets and wants, great confidence and obsession).

8. Remember, "That is the technique for things"

PRACTICE: Develop a Mind Control Plan to Control Anger (and Hostility)

1. Consider at any rate one anger conditions.
2. Use the above systems to make a psychological activity to vanquish anger right now.
3. Develop your own one of a kind psychological thinking once-over or plan (taking into account these procedures) what you will say when you explode.

Strategies for action to reduce anger.

1. Figure "hostility will make a hole between us"

Consider somebody who really or upsettingly trapped you. How was that experience? The dread, torment and anger about this memory can remain with you for a surprising extra segment. Hostility can make a little degree of propelling contempt and division among you and the individual who actuated the assault. Compromising vibe can incite lost conviction and an anticipated dread of being harmed once more.

A practically identical exercise can apply when you hurt somebody, think it or not. You can "condition" your partner to dread or charge you as opposed to regarding you! Dread and hatred are not flawless with adoration.

Is this kind of suffering guile what you truly need when you are verbally or genuinely directing towards somebody you care about? This can harm and partition your right hand even with a slight "tag". (This will evidently likewise expand the question.) The impact can be gigantically overstated with somebody touchy to assessment or anger.

Take a gander at the uncommon stop sign! Consider the results before you trap somebody or discussion about anger. Or then again perhaps, try empathy; recognize your best targets; and be peaceful and crucial.

Work on: Digging your nails into the instance of a relationship? Envision your anger in your most enormous affiliations. Do you by and large drive a little division among you and your loved one each time you hurt them? Consider this corner each time you have an enticement. Or then again perhaps, pick steady clarifications of anger, (for example, discussing appraisals and issues).

2. be dynamic and mission for reasonable reactions for everybody

In case you are angry with somebody, revolve around your guideline target all during your time by day life. - Maximize joy for you and others. Pick companionship and pleasure; in any case, when you are perturbed, fortify your higher self.

Focus on your fellowship. Go to the most significant bit of yourself and find that bit of yourself (your Higher Self) that really respects that other individual (that is, paying little mind to what he does). Focus on these opinions of affection and hope to find the right reaction for everybody. Endeavor to grasp his point of view and yours. If you understand how to win a triumph win deal, you'll get a "triple win": 1 -

meet your fundamental needs, 2 - execute your own absurd anger towards another, perhaps 3 pass on someone else to feel nearer to you ("win"). The most ideal approach to manage dispose of a foe is to make him an amigo!

3. Take "holding up time" in the event that somebody gets an excessive amount of agitated.

Watch your own feelings when you are in a disappointing condition. On the off chance that you see that you are starting to feel a lot of irritated, enthusiastic, or committed, take "holding up time." Standby time recommends you quit talking or set aside enough effort to think, quiet down and recover control. Holding up times can be persuading whether they last from one to five minutes. Extra time clarifying what you need or how you need to regulate someone else.

To rest, I could state, "I need about an opportunity to consider what we've discussed." I should proceed with our discussion [in a few minutes, a while later, etc.] "Someone else I would lean toward not to go, solicitation, and leave.

Moreover, if you find that the other individual is getting pointlessly aggravated and not managing the circumstance significantly, take some time. You can say a near thing as already or state, "It appears as though we're both vexed, and on the off chance that we can't discuss it significantly greater serenity, I'll need to rest."

Stop toward the start of the contention; don't hold up until it ends up hurting. Recognize breaks as frequently as conceivable as fundamental to keep things sensibly serene and profitable.

    4. Find supportive approaches to manage dispose of high vitality and feelings

You heard the enunciation "escape from anger" to dispose of it. Freud used the likeness of a steam pot that would detonate if centrality was not discharged. With a particular goal in mind, the resemblance is significant.

Anger causes a raised level of charging and criticalness improvement discharges it. Research has affirmed that anger prompts a perspective boggling eagerness and importance that can prop up for a considerable time portion or significantly more. Then, we are continuously arranged to reestablished anger. Centrality rehearses use essentialness and helps scatter this additional tendency. Thus, aside from inner systems for diminishing aggravation, it is fundamental to diffuse anger through importance works out. Give working a shot, strolling, running, playing sports, working out, or doing different vitality turns out, particularly those that cause you to feel much improved.

5. Pick significant articulations of anger (not implosion)

Different people keep taking Freud's likeness. They recognize that so as to dispose of their anger, they should "escape from antagonistic vibe" by accomplishing something ruinous or harming to someone else or something. Different people, including several directions, erroneously recognize that extreme or clashing articulations of anger are the best way to deal with "choose our anger." We have to "decline" a person or thing. Research has shown that this conviction isn't significant.

In all honesty, any centrality lead reduces anger by dissipating feelings. It is also evident that the following "positive supposition" improves ruinous lead. Regardless, fortifying solid direct construes that it will end up being a more grounded inclination. People who use convincing behavior to "dispose of anger" will, all things considered, be continuously strong as opposed to less ordering. Research verification bolster this end. A superior technique than decay anger is by accomplishing something significant and vivacious, for example, working out, playing sports, or partaking in something really incredible that manages the issue.

Shouldn't something be said about forceful "sensible" direct? In what limit may you feel if somebody called you "idiotic", "one-sided" or an enormous social occasion of different negatives and after that communicated, "I simply expected to talk reality with respect to how I feel." How may you feel how beneficial would she say she was for the relationship?

The convincing clarification may have been certified as he had educated his contemplations in a minute as for anger. By the by, was the circumstance generally speaking? Or of course, was his "validity" just a development of irate musings expected to hurt you with the target that you could see the mischief yourself?

Wouldn't it be significant for the other individual to uncover to you that he really considers you, in any case, is incensed about something you did? Wouldn't it be intelligently useful to an individual to set aside the push to look at their perspective and to scan for significant reactions for the issue? Which approach is great? Solid "validity" or reflexive and unequivocal unwavering quality?

PRACTICE 1: (1) List your crazy clarifications of anger and supplant them with helpful verbalizations. Once-over the propensities by which you administer puzzling conditions. What contemplations increment your anger? What words or activities trouble others, your affiliations, or yourself? (Models: holler, swear, snare, throw things, eat, smoke, eat up prescriptions, keep away from an issue, or accuse someone else). What experiences and activities would be ceaselessly useful?

(2) List vitality exercises to decrease anger. Sports, work out, biking, strolling, running, assignments, snickering and even (significant)

discussion would all have the alternative to decrease suppositions of anger. The more remarkable the advancement, the more possible it is.

PRACTICE 2: Develop a complete exchange off course of action (neither convincing nor torpid). Look for after the recommendation above to build up an arrangement for supervising dependably in conditions where you will when everything is said in done be angered and forceful (or not unequivocal). Journey for commonly beneficial approaches.

BRAINWASHING

This zone is going to center in travel toward brainwashing and the entirety of the parts that go with it. Through the media and the movies that are seen, different people consider brainwashing to be a mischievous practice that is done by the people who are trying to weaken, influence, and to gain power. Some who truly have faith in the power of brainwashing recognize that people including them are endeavoring to control their minds and their lead. Generally, the course toward brainwashing happens in a by and large progressively unobtrusive way and excludes the horrendous practices that enormous number people unite with it. This part will go into significantly more information concerning what brainwashing is and how it can influence the subject's perspective.

What is Brainwashing?

Brainwashing right currently is talked about like its use in psychology. At this moment, is recommended as a strategy for out and out considered change social impact. This sort of social effect is happening for the range of the day to each person, paying little notification to whether they get it or not. Social impact is the accumulating of procedures that are used so as to change others' practices, emotions, and tempers. For example, consistence frameworks that are used in the working environment could, really, be viewed as a kind of brainwashing since they envision that you should act and think a specific way when you are occupied with working. Brainwashing can wind up being, to a progressively conspicuous degree, a social issue in its most certifiable structure considering the way that these systems work at changing the manner by which someone thinks without the subject consenting to it.

For brainwashing to work successfully, the subject is going to need to experience a hard and fast separation and reliance because of its noticeable contact concerning the issue. This is one explanation that huge amounts of the brainwashing cases that are considered happen in totalistic religions or prison camps. The brainwasher, or the executive, must have the decision to increase endless oversight over their subject. This surmises they should control the dietary examples, snoozing structures, and satisfying the other human needs of the subject and none of these activities can happen without the hankering of the power. During this technique, the chairman will work to profitably confine the subject's entire character to fundamentally make it not work right any more. When the character is broken, the ace will work to abrogate it with the ideal sentiments, tempers, and practices.

The course toward brainwashing is still helpfully discredited whether it will work. Most clinicians hold the emotions that it is conceivable to intellectually program a subject as long as the correct conditions are open. Also, at last, the entire technique isn't as absurd as it is appeared in the media. There are in like way different implications of brainwashing that make it logically difficult to pick the impacts of brainwashing with respect to the issue. A piece of these definitions require that there must be a sort of hazard to the physical body of the subject to be viewed as brainwashing. On the off chance that you look for after this definition, by then even the practices done by different fan religions would not be viewed as clear brainwashing as no physical abuse happens.

Different implications of brainwashing will depend upon control and threatening without physical power to get the modification in the sentiments of the subjects. Notwithstanding, specialists recognize that the impact of brainwashing, significantly under the perfect conditions, is only a passing occasion. They recognize that the old character of the subject isn't totally obliterated with the preparation; rather, it is set into concealing and will return once the new character isn't fortified any more.

Robert Jay Lifton arranged some fascinating contemplations on brainwashing as for the 1950s after he reviewed prisoners of the Chinese and Korean War camps. During his observations, he concluded that these prisoners experienced a multistep system to brainwashing. This approach started with assaults on the notion of self with the prisoner and, starting their onward, finished with an alleged change in sentiments of the subject. There are 10 stages that Lifton depicted by the brainwashing system in the subjects that he investigated. These included:

1. A snare on the character of the subject
2. Forcing issue concerning the issue
3. Forcing the subject into self-shamefulness
4. Reaching a limit
5. Offering the subject opposition if they change
6. Compulsion to concede
7. Channeling the accuse the ordinary way
8. Releasing the subject of acknowledged issue
9. Progressing to comprehension
10. The last confirmation before a restoration

These stages must occur in a zone that is in finished isolation. This construes the vast majority of the conventional social references that the subject is familiar with interfacing with are difficult to reach. In addition, mind darkening structures will be used so as to quicken the procedure, for example, nonappearance of strong sustenance and nonattendance of rest. While this may not be considerable for all brainwashing cases, typically there is a closeness of a physical mischief which adds to the objective experiencing issues in speculation uninhibitedly and fundamentally like they normally would.

Steps Used

While Lifton isolated the strategies for the brainwashing system into 10 stages, present day consultants mastermind it into three phases so as to even more plausible handle what continues for the subject during this procedure. These three phases consolidate the separating of oneself, acquainting the opportunity of salvation with the subject, and the re-trying of the self of the subject. Seeing these stages and the system that occurs with every one of them can assist you with understanding what is coming upon the character of the subject with this methodology.

Separating of Self

The central time of the brainwashing strategy is fundamentally the separating of the. During this procedure, the manager needs to disconnect the old character of the subject so as to cause them to feel dynamically slight and open to the ideal new character. This development is fundamental so as to continue on the technique. The chairman won't be staggeringly profitable with their undertakings if the subject is still unequivocally set in their motivation and their old character. Separating this character and making the individual solicitation the things around them can make it less intricate to change the character in the later advances. This is done through two or three phases recollecting attack for the character of the subject, brining on issue, self-misleading, and some time later appears at the limit.

Ambush on Identity

The ambush on the character of the subject is fundamentally the specific assault regarding the issues' inclination of self, or their interior identity or character alongside their center game-plan of conviction. It makes the subject solicitation what their character is by causing them to envision that all that they have ever acknowledged isn't right. The professional will contribute a lot of essentialness denying everything that the subject is. In prisoner camps, for example, the manager will offer expressions like "You are certainly not making sure about circumstance," "You are not a man," and "You are not a warrior." The subject will be under ambushes like these consistently for a genuine long time up to months. This is done all things considered as to deplete the subjects with the target that they become astounded, befuddled, and depleted. Precisely when the subject appears at this sort of express, their emotions will begin to have all the reserves of being less strong and they may begin to recognize the things that they are told.

Fault

When the subject has experienced the ambush on their character, they will enter the time of deficiency. The subject will be constantly instructed that they are dreadful while experiencing this new character emergency that has been encouraged. This is done all things considered as to encourage an enormous estimation of issue to the subject. The subject will be continually persisting through an assault for any of the things that they have done, offering little appreciation to how colossal or little the showings might be.

The degree of the assaults can change moreover; the subject could be criticized for their conviction structures to the manner by which that they dress and even considering the way that they eat too bit by bit. After some time, the subject is going to begin to feel disregard around them continually and they will feel that everything they are doing aren't right. This can cause them to feel powerfully slight and slanted to oblige the new character the master needs to make.

Self-selling out

Since the subject has been convinced that they are dreadful and that a large portion of their activities are infuriating, the master is quitting any and all funny business to propel the subject to yield that they are awful. Directly, the subject is stifling in their own shortcoming and feeling confounded. Through the length of the psychological ambushes, the danger of some inconceivable physical insidiousness, or a mix of the two, the star will have the decision to drive the subject to blame his old character. This can join a wide combination of things, for example, getting the subject to accuse their own mates, sidekicks, and family who offer a near conviction framework as them. While this framework may require a tremendous stretch of time to happen, when it does, the subject will feel like he bamboozled those that he feels devoted to. This will develop the lack of regard comparably as the loss of character that the objective is beginning at now feeling, further separating the character of the subject.

Breaking point

By this point, the subject is feeling confined and confounded. They may introduce demands, for example, Where am I? Who am I? in addition, What may it be judicious for me to do? The subject is in a character emergency now and is experiencing some significant insolence. Since they have misled a large portion of the emotions and the people that he has continually known, the subject will experience a psychological crisis.

In psychology, this reasonable techniques a social occasion of certifiable appearances that consistently show a massive number of expected mental disturbing effects. A touch of the signs can fuse general confusion, significant wretchedness, and uncontrolled groaning. The subject may have the notions of being totally lost alongside having a free handle on this current reality. When the subject appears at this breaking point, they will have lost their opinion of self and the manager will fundamentally have the choice to do anything they need with them now since the subject has lost their comprehension of what's happening around them and what their personality is. In like way now, the ace will set up the different allurements that are significant to change over the subject towards another conviction structure. The new framework will be set up in a manner to offer salvation to the subject from the wretchedness that they are feeling.

Credibility of Salvation

After the ace has been convincing at separating the self of the subject, the open door has shown up to continue ahead to the going with organize. This development consolidates offering the subject the authenticity of salvation just if they are on edge to get some great ways from their past conviction framework and rather handle the overhauled one that is being advanced. The subject is allowed to comprehend what is around them, are instructed that they would be remarkable again and that they would feel extraordinary if they would simply look for after the new required way. There are four stages that are joined into this time of the brainwashing method; versatility, motivation to confirmation, planning of the shortcoming and discharging of the flaw.

Resistance

Resistance is the "I can engage you" to sift through. The subject has been confined and constrained to get some great ways from the people what's more, the sentiments that they have held for such a huge number of years. They have been taught that they are shocking and that all that they do isn't right. The subject is going to feel lost and in isolation on the planet, wretched at all of the loathsome things that they have done and contemplating what heading they can turn. Right when they appear at this stage, the manager can offer them a discharge by offering to support them.

This will occasionally be as an assistance from the abuse the subject has caused or some other little mindfulness. For example, the overseer can offer some additional sustenance or a refreshment of water to the subject or even take a few minutes to speak to the subject individual demands about home and friends and family. In the subject's current express, these little showings of liberality will appear, apparently, to be a significant encounter, accomplishing the subject inclination a significant slant of appreciation and help towards the star. As often as conceivable these emotions are way out of degree conversely with the contribution that has been made. In specific examples, the subject may feel like the ace has done the demonstration of sparing their life as opposed to simply contribution a little help. This mutilation of occasions works in the assistance of the ace as the subject is straightforwardly going to get ties of reliability with the manager as opposed to relics of past occasions.

Motivation to Confession

When the overseer has had the decision to get the trust of their subject, they will attempt to get a confirmation out of the system. This stage is as often as conceivable known as the "You can reinforce yourself." During this time of the brainwashing technique, the subject begins to see the complexities between the torment and accuse that they felt during the character ambush and the help that they are feeling from the unanticipated mercy that is advanced. In the event that the brainwashing strategy is astounding, the subject may even begin to feel a craving to respond a touch of the consideration that has been offered to them by the master. Right when this happens, the executive will have the choice to introduce the opportunity of confirmation as a potential technique to reducing the subject of the torment and accuse that they are feeling. The subject will by then be gone through a strategy of conceding the vast majority of the wrongs and sins that they have done heretofore.

Unmistakably, these wrongs and sins will be in association with how they sway the new character that is being made. For example, if the subject is a POW, this development will enable them to concede the wrongs that they did by securing possibility or doing fighting against the arrangement of the other nation. Regardless of whether these are less wrongs or sins, they battle with the new conviction framework that the framework is for every situation directly right now should be conceded.

Possessing of Guilt

When the subject enters the possessing of accuse advance, they have been experiencing the ambush of their self for a long time. When the subject shows up now in the brainwashing framework, they can feel the flaw and the disregard that has been put on them; anyway it has in every practical sense lost its significance. They are not set up to let you know unequivocally what they have destroyed to cause them to feel right now; simply comprehend that they are off base.

The executive will have the decision to use the away from of the subject so as to clarify why they are in the torment that they are feeling. The master will have the option in contrast to interface the assessment of accuse that the subject is feeling to anything they need. On the off chance that the chairman is trying to override a blueprint of emotions, they will take the old framework and convince the subject that those sentiments are what are causing them to feel the issue. This is the spot the comprehension between the old sentiments and the new emotions are grown; essentially, the old conviction framework has been set up to contrast and the psychological wretchedness that the subject has been feeling while the new conviction structure has been set up to relate with the capacity to escape from that devastation. The decision will be the subjects', anyway it is amazingly simple to see that they would pick the new structure to begin feeling much improved.

Discharging of Guilt

At the present time, subject has come to appreciate that their old attributes and sentiments are causing them torment. Presently they are depleted and tired of feeling the deficiency and irreverence that has been put on them for a long time. They begin to understand that it isn't for the most part something that they have done that causes them to feel along these lines; rather, it is their emotions that are causing the shortcoming. The tormented subject can feel some help from the way that there is something that they can do about the shortcoming. They will besides feel lightened considering the way that they eventually have gone to the understanding that they are not the horrendous individual, rather the people they have been close and their conviction structure that is the real guilty get-together that is causing the disquiet which is something that they can fix so as to wind up being unprecedented once more. The subject has discovered that they have far to get out just by getting away from a wrong conviction structure that they have held and understanding the redesigned one that is being advanced. All that the subject should do accordingly as to discharge the accuse that they are feeling is to condemn the foundations and people that are connected with the old conviction structure and after that they will be discharged from the shortcoming.

The subject starting at now has some request over this stage. They will have the decision to fathom that the presence of deficiency is up to them totally. All the subject should accomplish for this phase so as to be discharged from the unsoundness is to admit to any of the exhibitions they have given that are connected the old conviction framework. When the full confirmation is done, the subject will have finished the full mental rejection of their past character. The executive should step in now so as to offer another character to the subject and help them to re-try their character into the required one.

Fixing up of self

By this development, the subject has experienced a great deal of steps and lively disrupting impact. They have been overcome a fundamental that is relied upon to strip them of their old character, told that they are horrendous and should be fixed, and consistently go to the affirmation that their conviction framework is the explanation behind their beguiling quality and that it should be changed. When the greater part of this has been gone to, the subject is going to need to understand how to fix up their self, with the assistance of the manager. This stage permits the expert the opportunity to embed the contemplations of the new framework since the subject is a fresh start and amazingly eager to understand how to be and feel significantly better. There are two stages that are seen during this stage including concordance and the last confirmation before beginning eventually.

Congruity

The overseer will use this development to convince the subject that it is their decision to uncover an improvement. They may tell the subject that they have the decision to pick what is unprecedented and uncover an improvement that will assist them with feeling significantly better. The ace will by then present the new conviction structure and present it with the ultimate objective that makes it the phenomenal or the correct decision. During this sort out, the director will stop the abuse and rather have a go at offering the subject mental tranquil and physical solace. The reason for doing this is to change the old emotions to the desolation and enduring while at the same time modifying the new sentiments to satisfaction and help.

This stage is characterized up with the target that the subject is given the decision of which street to take, despite the way that it truly isn't up to them. The subject must use this phase to pick between the old sentiments and the new emotions, plausibly picking how they are going to feel for the remainder of their lives. By this point, the subject has as of late experienced the course toward reprimanding their old emotions considering the resistance and torment that they have experienced. In this way, probably, they will pick the decision for the new course of action of confidence so as to diminish their fault. The new character that has been demonstrated is engaging and safe since it is in no way, shape or form precisely proportionate to the old character that instigated the breakdown in before steps. Using premise and considering the perspective that the subject is in, it is less intricate to see that the essential character that the subject will decide for their own one of a sort real slants of serenity and security is the refreshed one.

Last Confession and Starting Over

Despite how the decision is truly not theirs using any methods, the overseer has intentionally worked the entire time to lead the subject to feeling like they have the absolutely chance to pick the new character. If the brainwashing framework is done decisively, the subject will think about the new decisions and set up that the best one is to take up the new character. They have been framed to think in this manner and in their new perspective, the one looks great. There are similar decisions; picking the new character engages them to be relieved from the accuse that they feel and prompts joy while picking the old character prompts torment and fault. If for some clarification the subject denied the new character, there would backtrack in the entire brainwashing approach and they would be constrained to experience everything again so as to wind up with the ideal outcomes.

During this period of the technique, the subject finds the opportunity to presume that they will pick extraordinary, which suggests that they get the chance to go with the new character. Right when the subject complexities the destruction and torment of their old character with the peacefulness that goes with the new, they will pick the new character. This new character looks like a kind of salvation. The thing makes them feel much improved and not have to oversee blame and melancholy any more. As this stage completes, the subject will reject their old character and will encounter a methodology of swearing reliability to their new one, understanding that it will work at improving their life.

Generally, there are administrations and customs that occur during this last stage. The change from the old character to the new character is a significant trial since much time and imperativeness has been used on the different sides. During these capacities, the subject will be acknowledged into the new system and got a handle on with the new character. For some brainwashing heartbreaking losses there is the conclusion of revival during this period. You are allowed to get a handle on your new character and are welcomed wholeheartedly into the new system that is by and by your own. As opposed to being separated and alone, you have various new associates and system people on your side. Instead of feeling the blame and misery that has tormented you for quite a while you are going to feel joy and quietness with everything that is around you. The new character is by and by yours and the brainwashing change is done.

This system can occur over a period of various months to even years. Most by far are set as a part of their character what's more, the feelings that they have; it is past the domain of creative mind to hope to change most of this in just several days with the exception of if the individual was by then prepared to change and that would make the brainwashing systems pointless. Detachment would in like manner be fundamental considering the way that outside effects will shield the subject from relying upon the administrator during this method. This is the explanation by far most of the brainwashing cases occur in prison camps and other isolated events; by a long shot a large portion of people won't get the chance of encountering brainwashing in light of how they are continually enveloped by people and advancement that would agitate the whole brainwashing process. When the individual is in detachment, the methodology takes a long time due to the various implies that must be taken in order to change the convictions held by the individual for quite a while so they will clutch the better approach for life as their own one of a kind while moreover feeling that the choice has reliably been theirs.

As can be seen, there are numerous advances that must be taken in order to encounter the brainwashing methodology. It isn't something that will happen just by running into someone in the city and exchanging a few words. It requires the imprisonment and time to convince the subject that all that they realize isn't right and that they are a dreadful person. It by then continues with endeavoring to control out an affirmation that the subject is horrendous and that they have to deny everything that they have done that are dreadful in light of their old character. Finally, the subject will be headed toward tolerating that they can improve if they just desert their old contemplations and rather handle the quietness and rightness that goes with the new character that is presented. These methods must occur for the brainwashing to be convincing and the new character to be set up. Brainwashing as Court Defense from the earliest starting point of time, people have been ensuring that they submitted awful wrongs since they had been influenced. It was an explanation that many would ensure needing to save their own lives or to pull off a mass murder or some other unspeakable barbarity. It might even be something as clear as taking from another person. Whatever the action was, brainwashing was a straightforward hindrance since it made the commitment of the move away from the charged and it was difficult to determine if someone had been mentally molded or not.

On account of brainwashing supplications can be used as a security in the court is up to some conversation. Various experts feel that by allowing this obstruction into the court, the courts would advance toward turning out to be overwhelmed with counterfeit instances of brainwashing and the benefits for showing or defaming this gatekeeper would be past what the courts could manage. Despite this, there have been a couple of cases brought to court that may show the authenticity of brainwashing as an opposition for bad behaviors submitted.

HYPNOSIS

While brainwashing is a bewildering kind of mind control that different people have pondered, hypnosis is likewise a fundamental sort that should be considered. For the most part, the people who consider hypnosis consider it from watching stage shows of people doing senseless acts. While this is a kind of hypnosis, there is fundamentally more to it. This region is going to concentrate more on hypnosis as a kind of mind control.

What is Hypnosis?

Regardless, is the massiveness of hypnosis? According to masters, hypnosis is seen as a condition of mindfulness that joins the pulled in thought near to the diminished periphery care that is portrayed by the part's comprehensive capacity to respond to proposition that are given. This prescribes the part will enter a substitute point of view and will be astonishingly continuously vulnerable against look for after the recommendations that are given by the surprise inducer.

It is conventionally seen that there are two hypotheses pack that help to outline what's happening during the hypnosis timespan. The first is known as the reasonable state speculation. The people who search for after this theory see that hypnosis takes after a stupor or a viewpoint that is changed were the part will see that their consideration is adequately not really equivalent to what they would discover in their standard mindful state. The unmistakable theory is the non-state speculations. The people who search for after this theory don't recognize that the people who experience hypnosis are going into different conditions of perception. Or of course perhaps, the part is working with the stun capacity to enter a kind of imaginative development foundation.

While in hypnosis, the part is thought to have more fixation and focus that couples together with another ability to unequivocally concentrate on a specific memory or thought. During this technique, the part is in like route orchestrated to polish off different sources that may incorporate them. The entranced subjects are thought to demonstrate a raised ability to respond to recommendation that is given to them, especially when these proposition start from the trance inducer. The system that is used to place the part into hypnosis is known as rest inciting selection and will join an improvement of recommendations and headings that are used as a kind of warm up.

There are different contemplations that are raised by the authorities concerning what the vitality of hypnosis is. The wide collection of these definitions starts from the course that there are basically such endless different conditions that go with hypnosis and nobody individual has an identical experience when they are encountering it. A section of the different ramifications of hypnosis by pros solidify the going with:

1. "A stand-apart occasion of mental fall away from the confidence," Michael Nash.

2. Ernest Hilgard and Janet Hilgard have written in unprecedented Significance about hypnosis and depict it has a course for the body to isolate from itself in another plane of mindfulness.

3. Sarbin and Coe, two comprehended social clinicians, have use the term of business theory to depict hypnosis. Under this definition, the part is envisioning the action of being enchanted; they are acting like they are mesmerized instead of truly being in that state.

4. According to T.X. Beautician, hypnosis is delineated at risk to the unmistakable nonhypnotic social parameters. Under this definition, the part will depict the endeavor inspiration and etching the condition that they are in as hypnosis since they have no other thing to call it.

5. Weitzenhoffer wrote in a bit of his past works about hypnosis. He conceptualized that hypnosis is a condition of improved suggestibility. In later pieces, he continued portraying the demonstration of hypnosis as "a sort of effect by one individual applied on another through the medium or office of proposition.

6. Brenman and Gill used the psychoanalytic thought of "break confidence in the association of the

psychological self view," to help delineate what hypnosis was about. Under this definition, the part is fretful to go under hypnosis and into the fair state since it helps their psychological self picture and improves them to feel.

7. According to Edmonston, a person who has experienced hypnosis is basically in a puzzle get together of removing up.

8. Spiegel and Spiegel have conveyed that hypnosis is fundamentally something that occurs in context on the commonplace most remote scopes of the part.

9. Erickson states that hypnosis is a balanced, internal supported and wonderful condition of working. The part is starting quite recently masterminded to work and ponders things around them. Regardless, they are in a not too bad state stood separated from their normal state.

There are different points of view and pronouncements that have been made about hypnosis. A couple of people perceive that hypnosis is genuine and are suspicious that the association and others around them will attempt to control their minds. Others don't have confidence in hypnosis at all and envision that it is basically fit deluding. Likely, the authenticity of hypnosis as mind control falls in some spot in the middle.

There are multiple times of hypnosis that are seen by the psychological framework. These three stages fuse affirmation, suggestion, and weakness. All of them is basic to the hypnosis approach and will be discussed further underneath.

Enrollment

The fundamental time of hypnosis is affirmation. Before the part encounters the full hypnosis, they will be familiar with the rest actuating affirmation framework. For a long time, this was recognized to be the strategy used to put the subject into their trancelike trance; at any rate that definition has changed some at the present time. A dash of the non-state examiners has seen this stage maybe in an astounding manner. Or on the other hand possibly they acknowledge this to be as the framework to broaden the people's requirements for what will happen, delineating the development that they will play, standing isolated enough to be accepted to focus the right way, and any of different advances that are required to lead the part into the right bearing for hypnosis.

There are a few determination systems that can be used during hypnosis. The most extraordinary and convincing frameworks are Braid's "eye obsession" technique or "Braidism." There are different assortments of along these lines of thinking including the Stanford Hypnotic Susceptibility Scale (SHSS). This scale is the most used instrument to look at the field of hypnosis.

To use the Braid determination systems you should search for after a few phases. The first is to take any object that you can find that is dazzling, for example, a watch case, and hold it between the inside, fore, and thumb fingers on the left hand. You should hold this thing around 8-15 killjoys from the eyes of the part. Hold the article some spot over the asylums with the objective that it makes a lot of strain on the eyelids and eyes during the framework so the part can keep up a fixed look on the thing constantly.

The unexpected virtuoso should then uncover to the part that they should concentrate their eyes consistently on to the thing. The patient will in like manner need to concentrate their mind absolutely on that specific article. They should not be allowed to consider different things or let their cerebrums and eyes wander or probably the framework won't be pivotal.

In a little while, the part's eyes will begin to create. With really additional time the part will begin to perceive a wavy improvement. On the off possibility that the part typically closes their eyelids when the inside and fore fingers of the right hand are given from the eyes to the thing, by then they are in the daze. If not, by then the part should begin once more; endeavor to admonish the part that they are to connect with their eyes to close once the fingers are passed on in an in every practical sense undefined progression back towards the eyes once more. This will get the patient to go into the changed point of view that is known as hypnosis.

While Braid stayed by his own structure, he saw that using the affirmation method for hypnosis isn't constantly basic for each case. Believe it or not, experts right presently have usually discovered that the decision framework isn't as basic with the effects of rest beginning suggestion beginning late suspected. After some time, indisputable different decisions and assortments of the boss trancelike affirmation framework have been made, in spite of the way that the Braid system is starting at as of late considered the best.

Proposition

The going with time of hypnosis is known as the suggestion mastermind. Unequivocally when hypnosis was first depicted by James Braid, the term of suggestion was not used. Or on the other hand maybe, Braid prescribed this stage as the demonstration of having the clever character of the part base on one central and uncommon idea. The way where that Braid did this was to empower or decrease the physiological working of the different locale on the part's body. Later on, Braid began to put legitimately more accentuation on the use of different non verbal and verbal sorts of recommendation to get the part into the trancelike point of view. These would consolidate using "waking recommendations" equivalently as self-hypnosis.

Another astounding subliminal virtuoso, Hippolyte Bernheim, continued moving the enhancement of the state of being of the procedure for hypnosis over to the psychological framework that contained verbal suggestions. As demonstrated by Bernheim, rest affirmation is the determination of a psychical condition that is exceptional and which will assemble the deficiency of the suggestion to the part. Regularly, he conferred, the spellbinding state that is induced will engage the suggestion, despite the way where this plausible won't be fundamental to start the shortcoming regardless.

Current subliminal treatment uses a gathering of recommendation outlines in order to be useful, for example, depictions, recommendations, slippery or non-verbal proposition, direct verbal suggestions, and obvious fascinating explanations and proposition that are non-verbal. A bit of the non-verbal recommendation that may be used during the proposition stage would join physical control, voice tonality, and mental imagery.

One of the partitions that are made in the sorts of recommendation that can be offered to the part fuses those suggestions that are passed on with underwriting and those that obviously despot in the manner.

Something that must be considered as for hypnosis is the separation between the missing and the mindful character. There are a few stupor pros who consider the to be of the recommendation as a framework for giving that is guided generally speaking to the keen character of the subject. Others in the field will see it the other way; they see the correspondence occurring between the professional and the normal or missing character.

Safeguards of the most vital motivation behind the line of thought included Bernheim, Braid, and different pioneers of the Victorian age. They perceived that the propositions were being tended to truly to the sharp bit of the subject's mind, as opposed to the unmindful part. Believe it or not, Braid goes further and truly depicts the presentation of trancelike impact as the related with suspected upon the suggestion or the telling idea. The fear of most by far that surprise pros will have the decision to get into their oblivious and cause them to achieve and think things outside their capacity to control is basically stunning consenting to the people who search for after this line of thinking.

The possibility of the mind has in like manner been the determinant of the different beginnings about proposition. The people who perceived that the reactions given are through the wild character, for example, by morals of Milton Erickson, raise the examples of using variation recommendations. Monstrous measures of this abnormal suggestion, for example, stories or depictions, will cover their run of the mill criticalness to cover it from the keen character of the subject. Subliminal suggestion is a sort of hypnosis that depends absolutely upon the theory of the indiscreet character. If the negligent character were not being used in hypnosis, this kind of suggestion would not be conceivable. The separations between the two social issues are extremely easy to see; the people who perceive that the recommendation will go on a fundamental level to the watching character will use direct verbal norms and recommendations while the people who perceive the proposition will go basically to the thoughtless character will use stories and analogies with made sure about repercussions.

In both of these speculations of figured, the part ought to have the decision to concentrate on one article or thought. This empowers them to be rushed toward the way that is required in order to go into the spellbinding state. Precisely when the suggestion mastermind has been done adequately; the part will by then have the decision to move in to the third stage, nonattendance of confirmation.

Shortcoming

After some time, it has been seen that people will respond unquestionably to hypnosis. A few people find that they can fall into a rest affecting amazement enough reasonably and don't have to put a ton of vitality into the framework in any way at all. Others may find that they can get into the rest enacting shock, yet basically after a drawn out time allotment and with some exertion. Still others will find that they are not set up to get into the entrancing trance and significantly after continued with endeavors won't land at their targets. One thing that supervisors have discovered intriguing about the powerlessness of different people is that this factor remains reliable. If you have had the decision to easily get into a trancelike point of view, you are presumably going to be a relative course for a superb residual part. Of course, if you have constantly experienced issues in showing up at the rest activating state and have never been hypnotized, by then likely, you never will.

There have been a few exceptional models made after some place in the scope of an opportunity to attempt to pick the nonappearance of protection of people to hypnosis. A pinch of the more masterminded criticalness scales endeavored to wrap up which level of shock the part was in through the conspicuous signs that were available. These would consolidate things, for example, the unconstrained amnesia. A section of the more present day scales work to check the degree of self-surveyed or watched responsiveness to the specific recommendation tests that are given, for example, the energetic suggestion of arm enduring nature.

According to the examination that has been done by Deirdre Barrett, there are two sorts of subjects that are considered especially open with the effects of rest affirmation. These two get-togethers combine dissociaters and fantasizers. The fantasizers will score high on the ingestion scales, will have the option to successfully polish off the augmentations right now without the use of hypnosis, contribute a colossal proportion of their centrality taking a gander at nothing specifically, and had irregular assistants

Self-hypnosis

There are several occasions, for example, when an ensured trance authority or other ace isn't open, when you may use the methodology of self-hypnosis. This procedure happens when an individual can entrance themselves, reliably using the technique of autosuggestion. The fundamental use for this procedure is for mindfulness and different individuals will perform it to lessen their estimations of pressure, quit smoking, or to get the inspiration they need to stop eating so a ton of trashy sustenance. While two or three people may have the decision to self-entrance themselves, many find that they need a sort of help with arriving at the changed state. This could combine hypnotizing accounts or even character machine contraptions to assist them with showing up at that state. Different spaces that you could use self-hypnosis for merge your general physical thriving, to relax up, and to get over stage dread.

Stage Hypnosis

Precisely when a huge number people consider hypnosis, they consider create hypnosis. This is a sort of enjoyment that will happen in a theater or a club before a social affair of spectators. The subliminal authority is a significant part of the time showed up as an exceptional performer and this support hypnosis is totally about mind control. In the start of the show, the trance inducer will endeavor to put the entire gathering under the modified state before picking certain people who meet the criteria to come up on the stage and experience diverse humiliating acts while the remainder of the social undertaking watches.

It is dark why organize hypnosis is so compelling regardless of how it is generally thought to be a mix of dubiousness, stagecraft, physical control, suggestibility, part affirmation, and mental components. All things considered, experts recognize that the part is essentially cooperating in a manner with the surprise inducer and giving a superior than normal show. These people might be on edge to do this since they should be in all the idea, the strain to satisfy others, and the inspiration to struggle with their own one of a kind silencers of dread make it simple to get the people to perform. A touch of the books that have been made by past stage shock inducers reinforce the believability of tricky and dishonesty and some are totally made out of phony hypnosis where private mutters where used the entire time.

Sorts of Hypnosis

There are a combination of sorts of hypnosis that the subject will have the decision to experience. Every one of them will work in genuinely various propensities and some of them work to help with different issues. Some might be logically fit to helping the subject to extricate up while others can assist more with weight decline or torment the authorities. This part will talk in all the more understanding regarding the various sorts of hypnosis that are open.

Standard Hypnosis

The most comprehensively saw kind of hypnosis that is used is known as standard hypnosis. During this procedure, the executive is fundamentally making suggestions genuinely to the subject's indiscreet character. This kind of hypnosis will work the best with respect to an issue who is known for persevering through the things that they are told and they don't speak to a great deal of solicitation. In the event that you keep on visiting an avowed subliminal position or buy a tape to do the system of self-hypnosis, you will experience the procedure of customary hypnosis. The explanation that this kind of hypnosis is so inescapable is considering the way that it doesn't take that much affiliation or preparing to understand how to do. The subliminal ace is simply should make a fundamental substance and show the subject. While this system will work very well on the individuals who perceive what's going on around them, it is deficient for the individuals who think from a general perspective and methodicallly.

Ericksonian Hypnosis

The going with kind of hypnosis to be examined is Ericksonian Hypnosis. This one is reasonably progressively all around considering the way that it will require the use of analogies and little stories. These are used so as to show the musings and suggestion that are required to the careless character. Disregarding the way that this technique will require somewhat more experience and preparing to do, it is an amazingly productive and surprising strategy to use. The explanation that it works so well is since it can dispose of the obstacle and blockage that the subject may have to the recommendation.

There are two guideline sorts of equivalent characteristics that will regularly be used right now hypnosis; isomorphic and interspersal. For the portrayal that is interspersal in nature, the heading that is clarified has been imbedded into the story and would not be satisfactorily found by the subject outside of their missing character. The other kind, isomorphic similitude, is somewhat continuously normal and offers headings to the unmindful character just by familiarizing a story with the subject that will offer an average near the end. The careless character will be skilled to pull in a sorted out relationship accomplice the sections that start from the story and the portions that go with the lead or issue circumstance.

An occurrence of an isomorphic depiction is the story "child Who Cried Wolf." Many watchmen will use this story to show their kids lying, particularly if their kid tells a great deal of untruths. In the wake of hearing the story, the missing character of the subject would see an equal between the relating lies and the kid who is in the story. They would see that lying may actuate a disaster and the youthful may be much progressively arranged to quit lying in the process in requesting to shield that calamity from happening.

Application Technique

Another sort of hypnosis is known as the embedded system. During this system, the daze star will identify with the subject an intriguing story. This story is required to help include and interface with the insightful character of the subject. It will also contain roundabout proposals that are disguised inside the story yet which will be perceived into the careless character of the subject. Through this story the shock genius will use process administers so as to sort out the thoughtless character of the subject to discover the memory that is required. This memory is commonly about taking in experience that is genuine from a past time. The daze ace will by then have the decision to apply that learning data to assist them with making changes to their present.

MANIPULATION

Brainwashing and hypnosis are the two sorts of mind control that effectively ring a bell. While these two are essential to understanding the working of mind control and how everything limits, they are by all record by all record not by any means the only decisions that are open. Honestly, there are others that can be used and are consistently more convincing right now than either brainwashing or hypnosis. These specific frameworks are ones that can be used in standard conditions, for example like in regular conversations an individual may have with others. While it isn't likely that an individual will be controlled or convinced to change immense emotions through conventional conversations, they can be convinced to change not so much clear nuances, for example, being convinced to buy treats from a nearby adolescent scout or to cast a surveying structure a specific course in a political decision.

The basic stress to recall over the going with three sorts of mind control is that they will without a doubt happen in a people's everyday nearness with the people that they know and trust. Evidently, an individual won't put their subject into separation or power them into a changed perspective in like way with brainwashing. Or then again perhaps they will use different methodologies with an extreme goal to change the way their subject thinks.

The three sorts of mind control that fit into this characterization consolidate control, effect, and confusion.

This territory will investigate control and how it can ability to change the way "the subject" thinks. While control may not put the person who is using the strategy in damages' manner or cause any approaching danger, it is set up to work in a confounding and mischievous manner to change the lead, perspective and perception that the masterminded subject has in regards to a specific theme or condition.

What is Manipulation?

The fundamental solicitation that is consistently introduced is what control is? At the present time will talk about control in the focal points of mental control, which is a social impact that attempts to change the practices or impression of others, or the subject, through cruel, beguiling, or insightful procedures. The controller is quitting any and all funny business to move their own one of a sort inclinations, by and large to the disadvantage of another, so most by a wide margin of their frameworks would be viewed as misleading, naughty, harming, and exploitative. While social impact itself isn't continually negative, when an individual or get-together is being controlled, it has the authenticity of causing them hurt.

Social impact, for example, by ethicalness of an authority attempting to convince their patients to begin getting sound affinities, is regularly seen to be something that is innocuous. This is considerable for any social impact that is fit for as to help those included to pick and isn't unduly coercive. Obviously, if someone is trying to get their own specific way and is using people without expecting to, the social impact can be hazardous and is all around looked plummeting on.

Mental or energized control is viewed as a sort of effect and motivation. There are different portions that can be joined into this sort of mind control, for example, tormenting and brainwashing. Generally, people will consider this to be coldblooded or puzzling in nature. The people who choose to use control will do in that limit so as to endeavor to control the direct of everybody around them. The controller will have some outrageous objective as a top need and will work through different abuse frameworks to constrain people around them into helping the controller locate a serviceable pace objective. Routinely fiery shakedown will be fused.

The people who practice control will use mind control, brainwashing, or annoying systems to get others to finish the undertakings for them. The subject of the controller most likely won't have any desire to play out the errand, yet feel that they have no other option because of the compulsion or other philosophy used. Most by a long shot who are manipulative don't have the most ideal minding and affectability towards others so they may not see an issue with their activities.

Different controllers simply need to locate a serviceable pace objective and are not worried over who has been vexed or harmed on the way.

Essentially, manipulative people are a significant part of the time reluctant to get into a strong relationship since they are frightful others won't remember them. Someone who has a manipulative character will routinely have the failure to anticipate hazard for their own practices, issues, and life. Since they are not set up to anticipate the hazard for these issues, the controller will use the procedures of control to get someone else to acknowledge control over the obligation.

Controllers are a significant part of the time arranged to use relative frameworks that are found in different sorts of mind control so as to get the impact they need over others. One of the most usually used frameworks is known as excited coercion. This is the detect the controller will work to rouse compassion or fault in the subject they are controlling. These two estimations are picked since they are viewed as the two most grounded of every human inclination and are the well while in travel to spike others into the action that the controller needs. The controller will by then have the choice to abuse the subject, using the compassion or accuse that they have made to pressure others into arranging or helping them appear at their last objective.

Sometimes, the controller won't just have the choice to make these opinions, they will have the decision to rouse degrees of sympathy or accuse that are way out of degree for the situation that is going on. This proposes they can take a condition, for example, abandoning a party appear as though the subject is deserting an internment administration or something that is very enormous.

Fiery investigation is only one of the methods that are used by controllers. One of different methods that has been gainful for specific, controllers is to use a kind of misuse that is known as insane making. This procedure is customarily pointed with the longing for making self-question in the subject being controlled; as often as conceivable this self-helplessness will end up being strong to the point that two or three subjects may begin to have emotions that they are going insane. Now and again, the controller will use sorts of isolated directing behavior so as to recognize insane making. They may in like way show backing or endorsing of the subject verbally, yet then offer non-verbal hints that show confining ramifications. The controller will routinely effectively try to undermine certain occasions or practices while displaying their help so anybody can hear for that equivalent lead. In the event that the controller is trapped in the appearing, they will use repudiation, sponsorship, defend, and cheating of incapacitated course of action so as to escape from the issue.

Possibly the best issue with mental controllers is that they are not continually arranged to perceive what others around them may need and they will lose the capacity to address or much thinks about these issues. This doesn't exculpate the immediate that they are doing, yet regularly the essentials of others are not considered or are not a need to the controller so they can perform manipulative undertakings without feeling fault or disapproval. This can make it difficult to stop the direct and clarify in a commonplace manner why the controller must stop.

Besides, the controller may find that it is difficult for them to shape significant and dependable family relationships and associations because the people they are with will dependably feel externalized and will experience issues in confiding in the controller. The issue goes the two novel courses in the strategy of associations; the controller won't have the decision to see the necessities of the other individual while the other individual won't have the decision to shape the basic enthusiastic affiliations or trust with the controller.

Necessities to Successfully Manipulate

A profitable controller must have methods near to that will make them beneficial at using people to locate a decent pace last objective. While there are two or three speculations on what makes a practical controller, we will investigate the 3 necessities that have been set out by George K. Simon, an effective psychology producer. As demonstrated by Simon, the controller should:

1. Be arranged to cover their convincing practices and wants from the subject.
2. Be arranged to pick the vulnerabilities of their typical subject or on the other hand abused people to comprehend which

techniques will be the best in appearing at their destinations.

3. Have some degree of mercilessness rapidly accessible so they won't have to manage any doubts that may rise because of hurting the subjects if it wraps up that way. This damage can be either physical or excited.

The fundamental that the controller needs to achieve all together to sufficiently control their subjects is to conceal their convincing practices and targets. If the controller evades telling everyone their game-plans or dependably acts intend to other people, nobody will remain adequately long to be controlled. Or on the other hand maybe, the controller ought to have the option to cover their musings from others and act like everything is normal. Consistently, the people who are being controlled won't get it, at any rate for no situation. The controller will be sweet, act like their closest companion, and potentially help them with trip with some issue or another. When the subject ponders the issue, the controller has enough information on them to oblige the subject into progressing forward.

Next, the controller should have the limit of comprehending what the vulnerabilities of their organized awful misfortune or abused people are. This can assist them with making sense of which methods should be used so as to appear at the general objective. A portion of the time the controller may have the decision to do this development through a touch of recognition while different occasions they are going to need to have a sort of relationship with the subject before thinking of the full arrangement.

The third need is that the controller should be barbarous. It won't turn out positively if the controller places in the aggregate of their work and, by then stresses over how the subject is going to reasonable at last. If they considered the subject, it isn't likely that they would continue with this strategy in any capacity whatsoever. The controller won't consider the subject at all and doesn't generally mind if any damage, either physical or lively, happens to the subject as long as the general objective is met.

One clarification that controllers are so convincing is that the subject as often as conceivable doesn't grasp they are being controlled until some other time simultaneously. They may feel that everything is coming alright; maybe they envision that they have made another accomplice in the controller. When the subject remembers they are being used or never again ought to be a touch of the method, they are gotten. The controller will have the choice to use a wide extent of strategies, including vivacious shakedown to get their direction at last.

Bit by bit directions to Control Victims

Something that the controller should have the decision to achieve to see achievement is to control their subjects.

There are two or three specific speculations that are available to help clarify how the controller will have the decision. Two of the hypotheses that will undoubtedly be broke down right now those began by Harriet Braiker and Simon.

Harriet Braiker is a clinical pro who has made a personal development manage. In her book, she has depicted five fundamental ways that the controller can control their subjects. These include:

Rousing information

Negative help

Halfway or uncontrollable help Discipline

Horrendous finding that as they say gives one fundamental

The hidden two strategies that are talked about fuse moving info and negative help. In motivating analysis the controller will use a collection of procedures, for example, open affirmation, outward appearances (like a grin or a constrained chuckle), consideration, favors, support, money, over the top saying 'sorry' shallow compassion which may consolidate fake tears, shallow interest, and honor. The reason for using this sort of post is to give the individual inspiration to ought to be your companion. If you give someone a gift or some money, they may be considerably progressively arranged to help you out when the open entryway appears. If you can cause the subject to feel perplexed about you, by then they will have the significant compassion to be your accomplice later. The other sort of stronghold that can be used is negative help. At the present time controller will remove the subject from a condition that is negative as a compensation for accomplishing something different. An occurrence of this would be "You won't need to finish your work if you engage me to do this to you."Each of these has express qualities and shortcomings that enable the controller to get what they look for from the subject. Typically, the controller will use a mix of different frameworks so as to get the things that they need.

Fragmentary or sporadic help can in like way be used by a controller. This kind of help is used so as to enough make a quality of helplessness and dread in the subject. An occurrence of this comes in betting. While the scholar may win from time to time, they are up to this point going to lose a type of money when in doubt, particularly in the event that they play for a long time. Notwithstanding, the triumphant is routinely enough to keep the subject continuing on a similar way, long after they are not set up to do along these lines. The controller will use this framework to offer help to the subject at enough interims to hold the subject returning.

Repelling is another procedure that is used in order to control the subject of the controller. There are numerous exercises that can fit into this class. They join playing the subject, crying, sulking, using the sorry fit, energetic coercion, swearing, dangers, and threatening, using the peaceful treatment, hollering, and troubling. The reason for using this strategy is to cause the subject to feel like they have achieved something inaccurately. The subject will feel horrendous and need to make things right, falling right back in with the controller.

At long last, the last system that Braiker makes reference to in her work is the horrendous one starter learning. This is the spot the controller will detonate for the most modest things with expectations of embellishment or setting up the subject into not wanting to disavow, go facing, or upset the controller. A portion of the procedures that might be used right now dangerous shock, unpleasant assault, and other conduct that is frightening and used to set up transcendence and quality over the subject.

Simon has in like way thought of a once-over of strategies that controllers must use so as to feasibly control their horrendous difficulties. A fragment of these look like those recorded by Braiker yet with two or three additional subtleties. These would include:

Lying: controllers are mind blowing at misleading their subjects. As often as could be expected under the circumstances, the subjects will find that it is difficult to provoke when they are being bewildered by then. Right when the subject finds a couple of solutions concerning the conspicuous misrepresentation, it is normally past where it is conceivable to do what should be done. The fundamental way that the subject can ensure that they are reducing their odds of being misdirected are paying special mind to different character types that are aces in the claim to fame of conning what's more, lying. The controller will lie about anything so as to get their path and generally their subjects won't have any thought that it is going on until it is past where it is conceivable to complete it.

Oversight lying: this one takes after the system recorded above with a few slight differentiations. Prohibition lying is somewhat progressively unobtrusive considering the way that the controller will confess all with some of yet will hold certain key issues that ought to have been uncovered. Once in some time this may be called introduction. The controller may communicate that they have to increase some money to get gas to go purchase staple product when in all honesty they need the money to go get several prescriptions or other unlawful substance. While they used the money to buy gas, much proportionate to the communicated, they neglected a basic part. The subject more than likely would not have given the money if they knew the completion of the story and now they might be up to speed in something unlawful.

Forswearing: controllers are experts at refusal. None of them will yield that they have accomplished something erroneously, in any occasion, when a large portion of the proof is pointing towards them. They will dependably preclude everything and much from claiming the time cause the subject to seem, by all accounts, to be the one to fault.

Legitimization: this is the place the controller will think about a resistance that makes them look mind boggling. They may state they basically did the show since they were attempting to help the subject. This framework is in addition identified with the methodology for turning.

Minimization: this is a mix of the legitimization and the refusal strategies. The controller will tell everyone that their direct is really not as dishonest or dangerous as the subject idea. A case of this would be the place the controller says that an assault or affront they performed was only a joke and that the subject ought not concentrate on it so.

Specific consideration or mindlessness: during this framework, the controller tries to avoid offering savvy concerning whatever will divert them from their last objective. They will trivialize it and cause it to show up not irrationally fundamental to them, which it truly isn't. An occurrence of this would be the place the controller says "I would lean toward not to hear it."

Distraction: controllers are not just unprecedented at deluding their subjects; they are besides specialists at staying away from contribution straight reactions to questions that are given to them. If someone asks them a solicitation that they couldn't think about or needs to know inside and out if they are misleading them, the controller will try to push the conversation toward another way. Routinely the controller will quickly offer an ill defined reaction to the solicitation before moving the conversation to another point.

Evasion: this procedure looks like redirection with a few complexities. At this moment, controller will respond to the solicitations that are given to them, anyway they will use weasel words, questionable responses, meander indiscreetly, and give superfluous responses to the solicitation. They will leave the subject with a greater number of solicitations than answers when they are done.

Compromising: The controller will dependably attempt to keep the hurt individual tense so as to ensure that they stay on a comparable assembling all through the technique. As often as conceivable this is done by using covered up, prompted, aberrant, or inconspicuous dangers to the subject.

Contrite fit: controllers like to use the apologetic fit as a kind of compromising so as to get the subject to do what they need. The controller will try to cause the subject to feel contrite, all things considered, for example, by saying that the subject has it unreasonably clear, is extremely narcissistic, or basically couldn't ponder the controller enough. This will understand the heartbreaking misfortune beginning to feel frightful for the controller. The subject will by then be kept in a satisfying, excited, or self-questioning position, making it less difficult for the controller to at present use them.

Disfavoring: the entire objective of the controller is to cause the subject to feel horrendous or have sympathy toward them so the subject props up alongside the course of action. One way that the controller can do this is by using managed downs and joke to slight the subject. This system will cause the subject to feel disgusting. A colossal fragment of the affronting frameworks used will be unobtrusive and would fuse things, for example, honest joke, consistent remarks, shocking method for talking, or a wild look.

Rebuffing the subject: this is one of the most overarching systems that can be used considering the way that it will in a concise minute put the subject busy working of block while at a practically identical time camouflaging the controllers exceptional targets. The controller will attempt to turn the conditions around with the target that the subject appears as though they are the rapscallion and the person who has raised a large portion of the free for all. The subject will by then need to discover approaches to manage change this point and ricochet on the controller once more, making it simple to be used.

Representative work: controllers will a significant part of the time cover their own courses of action by making it appear as though the work they are doing is for some respectable reason. They just said the mean thing as for your outfit considering the way that the principle needs to fire tidying up the nearness of the school and they expected to help. The articulation "simply finishing my obligation," would in like way fit under this class.

Enchantments: controllers can use allurement to get the things that they need. Two or three devices that fit into this class would consolidate phenomenal help, smooth talk, recognition and guarantee. This is done in that capacity as to get the subject to chop down their gatekeepers. After time, the subject will start to give their devotion and trust to the controller who **will use it anyway they see fit**.

Indicating stun: when the controller uses stun, it is to get the subject to feel sorry or compassion toward them. Whenever done in the correct manner, the controller will have the decision to amaze their subject again into settlement. Routinely, the controller isn't commonly angry; they are basically managing on an appearing to get what they **need.**

As can be seen, there **is a great deal** of instruments that the controller can use so as to locate a decent pace objectives. Typically, these frameworks will be used with the objective that the subject won't understand what's happening before all else and it will require some endeavor for them to bounce on. When they do, the controller will have the decision to use a piece of the frameworks that will be talked about in the going with zone so as to prop the subject up the correct way. The controller is able at using a blend of these abilities to get the things that they need and it doesn't have any sort of impact to them the entirety they hurt the other individual simultaneously.

As talked about effectively, a controller is quitting any and all funny business so as to appear at their last objective. To appear at this last objective, the controller will use any framework that they can so as to get people to do what they need. The five most standard procedures that will be used by a controller to appear at their last targets fuse coercion, passionate investigation, putting down the other individual, lying, and making a dream. These will each be **talked about in the past sections.**

Coercion

Coercion is the basic framework that would be used by a controller. Investigation is viewed as an exhibition that consolidates dangers that are unjustified so as to make a specific expansion or cause an episode to the subject with the exception of if the controller's preferred position is met. It can also be depicted as the demonstration of weight that fuses dangers of arraignment as a guilty party, dangers of taking the subject's property or money, or dangers of making physical mischief the subject. There is a long history of the word coercion; from the outset it was a term that proposed portions that the voyagers rendered to the zone that was flanking Scotland to the chieftains in control. This portion was made so as to give the pioneers security from the privateers and punks that were going in to England. It has since changed to mean an option that is other than what's normal and in unequivocal cases it is an offense in the United States. For the explanations behind this region, coercion is to a progressively conspicuous degree a danger, either physical or passionate, to the subject to force them into doing what the controller needs.

Extortion is in like way observing as intimidation from time to time. Despite the path that there are times when the two are viewed as synonymous, there are several differentiations. For example, coercion is the place someone takes the individual property of another by figuring out how to do future damage if the property isn't given. Obviously, investigation is when dangers are used so as to shield the subject from participating in genuine exercises. Once in some time, these two occasions are quitting any and all funny business together. The individual may undermine someone and require money so as to be monitored and not **cause the subject wickedness.**

The controller will be set up to use this framework to get what they need. They are going to set aside the push to learn things of individual nature about their subject and a brief timeframe later they can use that as a kind of investigation against them. They may investigation their subject by figuring out how to spill a mortifying riddle or by demolishing their odds of finding a different profession or progress. Or on the other hand the controller may work in an all the all the all the more undermining course by making moves to truly hurt their subject or the subject's family if they don't consent to oblige the controller. Whatever the extortion might be, it is used to assist the controller with finding a serviceable pace objective with the help of the subject.

Passionate Blackmail

Another equivalent philosophy that might be used by the controller is known as passionate coercion. During this procedure, the controller will endeavor to move compassion or fault in their subject. These two conclusions are the most grounded ones for people to feel and they will routinely be sufficient to spike the subject into the development that the controller needs. The controller is going to misuse this reality so as to get what they need; they will use the compassion or the accuse that they convince so as to urge the subject in to taking an intrigue or helping them. The level of sympathy or accuse will as often as conceivable be made a colossal course of action about, making the subject considerably bound to help the condition.

The motivation behind using this sort of coercion is to play more on the slants of the subject. In typical extortion, the subject has a danger to regulate, by and large with respect to physical deviousness to themselves or someone they love. With passionate coercion, the controller will work to rouse feelings that are sufficiently prepared to induce the subject to action. While the subject may feel that they are aiding of their own totally opportunity, the controller has tried to guarantee that they subject is helping and will draw out the emotions again at **whatever point it is required**.

Manipulation is a kind of mind control that is difficult for the subject to avoid. Not at all like brainwashing and hypnosis that was delineated in the past sections, manipulation can occur in step by step life and in specific examples it can occur without the subject having a great deal of learning or control of it. The controller is getting serious discretely in order to show up at their last target without getting the subject suspicious and wreck the technique. The controller won't worry over **whom** they are hurting or how others may feel and most by far of them are not fit for understanding the necessities of their subjects. They essentially understand that they need something and that the subject they have picked is going to help them with finding a workable pace.

The strategies that are discussed right now planned to help clarify what continues during the technique of manipulation and how the cerebrum of the controller will work. It is consistently best to try to maintain a strategic distance from any person who might be a controller with the objective that you can avoid this kind of mind control.

CONCLUSIONS

Presently, the opportunity has arrived to derive from these observations that social principles, laws, and morals are in truth "run of the mill" for people, and that society consistently powers pack behavior on them reliant on what is historic stood out from the desperate. In all honesty, this perseverance mindset is our standard and society really endeavors to control the wild mammoth in every person by ensuring that since the starting it agrees to the laws, rules and morals of the dominating get-together, when in doubt the rich, who overpower our governing bodies and our establishments. That is the explanation we ought to censure the people who acknowledge that society doesn't offer them sensible treatment: what, in fact, would it be a smart thought for them to do to get by in a much of the time hostile condition where advantage depends upon their school, your family or your riches? Psychology itself must leave the storeroom and perceive that run of the mill human behavior must be against firm social requests and rules. In all honesty, people are incensed with society, yet since they are weak against the people who control institution and morals, they feel powerless about expecting to live among sheep. Is it surprising that sporadically it happens that a disengaged individual chooses to change society or his condition to lead an increasingly freed and best controlled life over the mercilessness of a society that, as we have seen, ends up disintegrating and envisioning oneself as the new rich and fantastic recovering control. In the main outstanding century, we have seen China move from a store directed area to a military framework controlled by the rich and stunning, to a communist outlook during the 1950s when Marxism would choose a lone life for everybody in conclusion, China today as a business visionary communist state subject to the choice a social occasion that describes the lives of an exposed people, which has genuinely struggled to oversee over the rulers as much as the Emperor of years past - nothing has changed aside from the rich and earth shattering. There will be another uprising in China later on - presently it seems, by all accounts, to be outlandish notwithstanding the disturbance in various bits of China, caused by minorities being constrained to follow the central law. Not all domains can see their own disappearing! So by what means will psychology address this issue of human behavior as a fundamental continuance part, to be specific that people are typically horrible, severe, and beating others more powerless than them? Psychiatry in mental clinical centers is routinely observed as techniques for social control. In case you don't agree with society and its standards, you ought to be crazy. Right now, should partake and be in control for the security and preferred position of all. Psychology, on the other hand, has all the earmarks of being a liberating some portion of mental prosperity: we help people who are out of coordinate with society discover their place and discover behaviors that they consider common at this moment. Where will the people who oppose the society wherein they live and need another lifestyle respond without intruding with the amazing and the chance to continue with the presence they choose for themselves? Or then again do we believe that movies will become reality, a disaster that envisions all people and an appearance to being a dog is called perseverance, the real social standard!